Twayne's United States Authors Series

Sylvia E. Bowman, *Editor*

INDIANA UNIVERSITY

Julia Peterkin

TUSAS 273

Julia Peterkin

JULIA PETERKIN

By THOMAS H. LANDESS
University of Dallas

TWAYNE PUBLISHERS

A DIVISION OF G. K. HALL & CO., BOSTON

Library of Congress Cataloging in Publication Data

Landess, Thomas.
  Julia Peterkin.

  (Twayne's United States authors series; 273)
  Bibliography: p. 156–58.
  Includes index.
  1. Peterkin, Julia Mood, 1880-1961.
PS3531.E77Z75   813'.5'2 [B]   76-13580
ISBN 0-8057-7173-5

MANUFACTURED IN THE UNITED STATES OF AMERICA

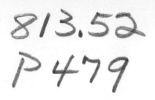

FOR MARY BETH

Contents

About the Author

Thomas H. Landess, Associate Professor of English at the University of Dallas has published over fifty poems and articles in such journals as *Sewanee Review, Georgia Review, Mississippi Quarterly,* and *Southern Review.* His critical commentary has been devoted primarily to Southern poets and fiction writers of the twentieth century; and his bibliography includes studies of the works of Eudora Welty, Caroline Gordon, Allen Tate, Andrew Lytle, James Dickey, and Shelby Foote. He has also written on such diverse figures as Thomas Merton, Mona Van Duyn, William Meredith, James Wright, Marion Montgomery, John Berryman, and Samuel Taylor Coleridge.

In addition to shorter studies, Professor Landess has published a monograph on contemporary novelist Larry McMurtry—*Larry McMurtry* (Austin: Steck-Vaughn, 1969)—and has edited a volume of essays on the fiction of Caroline Gordon, *The Short Fiction of Caroline Gordon* (Dallas: University of Dallas Press, 1973). At present he is working on a full-length critical study of the poetry of James Dickey.

His interest in contemporary poetry has led him to take part in the organization and administration of such projects as the Converse College Writing Workshop, the Southern Literary Festival, and the Agrarian Reunion; and he is presently serving on the staff of the Caroline Gordon Program of Creative Writing at the University of Dallas, where he teaches courses in contemporary literature and the techniques of poetry.

Born in 1931, he received his Bachelor of Arts and Master of Arts from Vanderbilt University and his Doctor of Philosophy in English from the University of South Carolina. While teaching at Converse College, Julia Peterkin's alma mater, he first became interested in her work and undertook the present study.

Preface

The period between World War I and World War II undoubtedly produced the most significant fiction in the history of American letters, and by the late 1920's Southern novelists and short story writers were beginning to receive respectful attention from critics and scholars in national as well as regional journals. Among those whose works won early acclaim was Julia Mood Peterkin, a South Carolina woman whose name was mentioned frequently along with that of William Faulkner, of Katherine Anne Porter, and of others as representing the highest achievement in the so-called Southern Renaissance. Since World War II, other names have been added to the list; but Mrs. Peterkin's has been all but forgotten; most of her fiction is out of print and largely ignored both by critics and by literary historians.

This study is primarily designed to correct the present errors of those who would casually classify her with local colorists and Old South apologists—categories which she herself regarded with undisguised contempt. Working quietly in the lengthening shadows of a social order she neither condemned nor condoned, she tried to render for a literate readership the timeless experiences of human existence as repeated by the Gullah Negroes of the South Carolina Low Country, a people whom she knew and understood from years of sharing their lives as she worked with them on her husband's plantation.

Her works, when they first appeared, provoked praise and admiration from members of the literary community, both liberal and conservative, both black and white. Indeed, her only detractors were the regional apologists with whom she is now being equated. Yet in the 1970's the seriousness of her intentions and accomplishments must be defended with the kind of close textual examination to which her peers and masters have been subjected. For this reason, the chapters of this book are largely devoted to a careful reading of her major works, including her four volumes of fiction and her collection of essays, *Roll, Jordan, Roll.* Chapter 1 is concerned with her life and times, and Chapter 7 is an evaluation of her place in the larger frameworks of Southern and American literature; but the burden of the study is a vindication of Mrs. Peterkin's reputation by submitting her to the same standards so often applied to Faulkner, Porter, and others who have been generally recognized as masters of their craft. At times, Mrs. Peterkin fails to measure up, but at times she succeeds admirably. Indeed, some of her fiction is so carefully and ingeniously wrought that it ranks among the finest in the literature of the twentieth century. And, for anyone with a taste for the grotesque, she supplies more than enough perversity and horror, most of which is as artistically functional as such analogous elements in the novels of Thomas Hardy and Flannery O'Connor.

If this seems high praise, it is offered in the belief that Mrs. Peterkin may eventually emerge as an important figure whose value, both as a portrayer of the black experience and as a fictional craftsman, will be widely acknowledged among critics who regard literature as something more than a weapon to be used in current social struggles. She sought all her life to avoid such struggles and to portray the Gullahs as they really were. Someday the majority of her readers may realize that such fictional treatment is the ultimate in justice and love.

THOMAS H. LANDESS

Acknowledgements

For permission to quote from unpublished letters I am indebted to William G. Peterkin, Jr., and William G. Peterkin, III, and to Edward Krickel. Also, Professor Noel Polk kindly supplied me with the frontispiece photograph. I would also like to thank the *Mississippi Quarterly* and The Southern Studies Program of The University of South Carolina for permission to reprint portions of this study.

The manuscript for this volume has been examined and criticized by several people, among them Professors M.E. Bradford and Louise Cowan of the University of Dallas and Professor Sylvia Bowman of the University of Indiana. Professor Bowman has been particularly helpful and patient in her proofreading and editorial comments. Her suggestions have almost invariably resulted in a better manuscript.

My greatest debt, however, is to Professor James B. Meriwether of the University of South Carolina whose knowledge and scholarship have been my most valuable allies in the considerable revision of a disquieting first draft. If any errors of fact still remain in the text, they undoubtedly crept in after his careful reading.

Finally, I wish to thank Sister Joseph Marie and the other staff members of the University of Dallas Library, all of whom helped me obtain obscure materials from places as foreign and strange to them as the libraries of South Carolina.

Chronology

1880   Julia Mood born October 31 in Laurens County, South Carolina.

1896   Graduated from Converse College, Spartanburg, South Carolina.

1903   July, married William Peterkin.

1921   Sketches appeared in the *Reviewer*.

1923   November, "Venner's Sayings" published in *Poetry: A Magazine of Verse*.

1924   *Green Thursday* published.

1925   Joined poetry society of South Carolina. "Maum Lou" won seventh place in *O. Henry Memorial Award Prize Stories of 1925*. Wrote "Whose Children?" by special request for inclusion in Alfred A. Knopf's anniversary edition, *The Borzoi, 1925*. "Vinner's Sayings" published in *Poetry: A Magazine of Verse*. Studied at Tours in France.

1927   May, awarded honorary doctor of letters degree from Converse College. Spent summer (by invitation) at MacDowell Colony in New Hampshire writing *Scarlet Sister Mary*. *Black April* published.

1928   October 26, *Scarlet Sister Mary* released.

1929   May 13, *Scarlet Sister Mary* announced as Pulitzer Prize–winning novel. June 13, Ethel Barrymore, the Schubert office, and Daniel Reed signed contract for stage rights to *Scarlet Sister Mary*.

1930   September 26, play opened Hartman Theatre. November 25, New York opening at Barrymore Theatre.

1932   February, Columbia, South Carolina, Julia Peterkin opened in *Hedda Gabler*. Met William Faulkner in Hollywood. Refused lecture series suggested by Bobbs-Merrill. *Bright Skin* published.

1933 *Roll, Jordan, Roll* published. Addressed Southern Women's National Democratic Organization in New York City.
1936 Spoke at Bread Loaf Inn Writers Conference, Ripton, Vermont. Taught at Bennington College in Vermont. Gave *New York Times* National Book Fair Speech.
1961 August, died, Orangeburg, South Carolina. Buried at Fort Motte, South Carolina.

CHAPTER 1

The Chatelaine of Lang Syne

ON cursory examination, the literary career of Julia Peterkin seems miraculous. When she began to write, she was already a woman in her forties— a wife and mother who was almost totally preoccupied with the responsibilities of her family and with the management of a large South Carolina plantation. As a student she had shown little or no interest in writing; indeed, she once confessed to an interviewer[1] that her sister had composed most of her college themes in exchange for coaching on mathematics. And, though in earlier years she did devote some time and energy to amateur theatrics, she had not yet become a member of the Charleston Poetry Society, nor did she meet with a monthly book club to discuss the latest best sellers, as many of her friends must have done.

Then the "miracle" occurred; and within a decade she had become one of the most celebrated novelists of her day, had won a Pulitzer Prize, and in a small way had helped to pioneer the harsh brand of Realism that was to become the characteristic idiom of twentieth century fiction. A closer examination of her early life, however, reveals that her phenomenal career was no miracle but the result of profound influences that amply prepared her to make her unique and significant contribution to American literature. The seeds of her success were planted during childhood and lay dormant in the darkest regions of her imagination while the years passed and her life ran its relatively uneventful course. Then the storm broke, and the growth began.

I Early Life

Julia Mood Peterkin was born in Laurens County, South Carolina, on October 31, 1880—the daughter of a highly esteemed physician, Julius Mood. Her mother, Alma Archer Mood, died shortly after her birth; and Julia was reared by an old Gullah[2] nurse, or "Mauma," who taught Julia the peculiar and marvelous speech of the black community even before she learned the "proper" speech of the South Carolina gentry. In addition to their language, she also absorbed many of the customs, superstitions, and attitudes of the Gullahs; and, like many another Southern child of her era, she undoubtedly saw life with the double vision of one whose sensibilities are conditioned for a time by two separate worlds. When alone with her nurse, for example, she spoke the Gullah patois, a curious speech almost unintelligible to the outsider; when she was in the presence of her white elders and on special behavior, she spoke a language acceptable to such company. Thus, from her earliest years, she was close to the Gullah world; and her tongue was adapted to the improbable diction and syntax of the Gullah dialect. It is unlikely that anyone exposed to those peculiar speech patterns in adult years could have developed the fine ear for them that Julia later displayed in her flawless dialogue.

Although she was in the custody of her Gullah "Mauma" during those early years, her father was still the most important person in her life; and his influence on her later career as a writer cannot be underestimated. Dr. Mood was the epitome of the country doctor—a man who was not only physician to all but also an intellectual and cultural leader in the scattered community of the rural up-country. As such, he was an amateur man of letters and the founder of the Fortnightly Club, a literary group that met to hear papers significant enough to be reprinted in *The State*, a newspaper which, along with the Charleston *News and Courier*, served the cultural needs of the entire state in lieu of any significant literary journals.

Dr. Mood was, from the beginning, Julia's most severe critic; he insisted that, even as a child, she maintain the highest standards of speech and behavior. In later years, after she had become a successful, if highly controversial, novelist, it was her father whom she most desired to please. All the critical praise that was lavished on her by the great and the near great never quite compensated for the fact that he seldom if ever gave his wholehearted support to anything she wrote.[3]

When she was ready for college—at an age when most girls are hardly out of junior high school—he sent Julia, along with her sister Laura, to Columbia College in the state capital where, for reasons that remain obscure, the two young ladies were utterly miserable. Already rebellious, Julia conspired with Laura to promote such mischief that they were both shipped home before the end of their first year. Dr. Mood, however, was waiting for them with an adamant heart; and they were not even allowed to unpack but were immediately dispatched to Converse College, a new institution just established at Spartanburg, South Carolina, by a wealthy millowner who could not bear to send his daughter to school in the far-off North. There the girls were quite happy; and, when Julia received her Bachelor of Arts before the age of sixteen, her father insisted that she stay in school in order to earn the degree of Master of Arts since he felt it would be risky to expose her to the world before she had gained some maturity.

At the end of her additional year, however, she again became rebellious; for, contrary to her father's wishes, she obtained a teaching position at Fort Motte, South Carolina, a rural farming settlement below Columbia which could offer her only a one room school house and fewer than ten pupils. The principal occupation of the community was farming; and the most prominent people engaged in that pursuit were the Peterkins. This family for generations had owned and operated Lang Syne Plantation, a pre-Revolution holding famous for its rich land and its wise management. This plantation remained largely intact—a rarity in South Carolina where Sherman's army and the economic hardships of Reconstruction had taken their toll.

Julia, by then a tall and strikingly beautiful woman with flame-red hair, soon caught the eye of William Peterkin, the young heir of the plantation; and, after a courtship of suitable length, they were married in July, 1903. Despite the fact that she was reared in an essentially rural environment, Mrs. Peterkin was totally unprepared for the responsibilities that fell to her as "chatelaine" of Lang Syne. Contrary to popular mythology, the life of a plantation owner's wife was not one of leisure and self-indulgence. Although she had servants to cook and tend to the household chores, she was expected to serve the blacks—between four and five hundred—who lived on the place and cropped for shares. These people looked to her for assistance with all the problems of their daily living, whether agricultural, medical, or personal. She was expected to "dominize" everything in sight from the moment she set foot on the threshold of the "Big House," and at the beginning she felt woefully inadequate.

For one thing, the blacks, all Gullahs and ex-slaves or the descendants of slaves, were born into the life of the plantation and were trained to perform the various tasks necessary to the survival and prosperity of the community. They knew when and how to harrow, plow, plant, and harvest; and they also knew what danger signals to heed in order to circumvent natural disaster. They could attend the birth of animals; raise them; when the time came, slaughter them with skill and ease; and make certain that nothing was wasted that could be put to good use.

Living close to nature, they also knew the flora and fauna of the woods and the fields that surrounded the settlement; and this extensive knowledge, derived from keen observation and superstition, was a source of constant admiration to the new mistress, who began to learn from them with much of the same humility that her young students must have learned from her. Because she had a searching mind and because she needed to know the people for whom she was responsible, she memorized a wealth of black lore, some of which she undoubtedly heard for the first time on Lang Syne. After the birth of her only child, William, Jr., her chief instructor was Maum Lavinia Berry, William's nurse and an ancient Gullah woman who became the model for Maum Hannah in three of Julia's most successful works of fiction.

While Mrs. Peterkin was learning the vocation of farming, she also led a full social life; took occasional trips to Europe; held active memberships in the Daughters of the American Revolution, the United Daughters of the Confederacy, the Afternoon Music Club, and other cultural organizations. She also grew roses; raised Llewellyn setters, pigeons, white Holland turkeys; embroidered; and experimented with horticulture. She obviously harbored tremendous creative energies that needed some outlet, but no evidence exists that she ever considered writing fiction. The literary propensities of her father, her impulse for self-expression, her treasure store of subject matter—all of these things remained dormant within her during the early years. Because her life seemed rich, productive, and thoroughly satisfying, her future at the age of forty must have seemed clear and secure.

II   *The Beginnings of a Literary Career*

Her literary career, it seems, was an accident born of personal tragedy and scrupulous conscience. After years of peaceful existence on Lang Syne, a series of misfortunes overtook her that might have broken the will of a weaker woman. Instead, it awakened in Mrs. Peterkin a sense of responsibility to life that culminated in a Pulitzer Prize and in worldwide fame. The trouble began when her husband suffered a ruptured appendix with complications and became a semi-invalid for the remainder of his life. This illness placed the responsibility of running the plantation squarely on his wife's shoulders, a burden which she might well have borne, all other things being equal.

But she had more trouble to bear. The Lang Syne hogs were stricken with a fatal illness; and the black foreman of the plantation, on whom she principally relied for aid and advice in running her affairs, contracted dry gangrene in his legs and was helpless at a time when she most needed him. Mrs. Peterkin, in an attempt to stimulate the circulation in his stricken limbs, brought a mild disinfectant to his cabin and prepared a hot foot bath. The disease, however, had already done irreparable damage; and, instead of a cure, her efforts produced what may have been for Mrs. Peterkin the moment of supreme horror. As the foreman sat with his feet in the milky white liquid, she saw his toes suddenly rise to the top and float loose on the surface. They had rotted away from his feet.

Old Dr. Mood was called in; and eventually he had to amputate both of the man's legs; but, though his life was spared for a short while, the foreman soon died, leaving Mrs. Peterkin bereft and tortured by lingering guilt. As she told a reporter years later,

It seemed to me that everything in the world had gone wrong, and I felt a sense of personal responsibility, as though I had got out of touch with the creative forces or had gone against the rules of the game, else I would have had the inner strength to meet these problems as they came. Perhaps being so closely associated with Negroes over a long period of time has influenced my own viewpoint. They have such strong faith and it gives them incredible courage and fortitude. And there is something that runs the show, call it what you will. We all have our marching orders. The humblest mud puddle in the road knows the moment the thermometer reaches 32, and turns into ice crystals.[4]

In this moment of self-examination Mrs. Peterkin concluded that she had somehow failed to live up to her own capabilities; and, remembering a long-discarded ambition to be a concert pianist, she resolved to resume music lessons as "a way out" of the emotional crisis with which she was confronted. This solution is a significant index of her character, for such a mechanistic view of the universe, curiously coupled with a sense of personal responsibility (what she called "that censor which I suppose we all have inside"[5]), undoubtedly came from Dr. Mood—both a scientist and a student of the humanities. This same combination of cold objectivity and conscientiousness was to manifest itself in all that she wrote, and her Realistic depiction of black life grew from such a disciplined vision.

Having made up her mind to study music once again, she engaged a piano teacher, Dr. Henry Bellamann, who was then an instructor forty miles away at Chicora College in Columbia. Once again fate had nudged her in the direction of literary fame; for Bellamann, in addition to teaching music, was also a writer of fiction whose novel *King's Row* became a best seller in 1940. In interviewing his new pupil, Dr. Bellamann expressed curiosity about her desire to return to music after so many years; and she told him the story of her soul-shaking experience with the foreman. Intrigued with Mrs. Peterkin's narrative gift and with her wealth of subject matter, Dr. Bellamann suggested that she write an account of the incident, partially as a means of purgation. Always modest in her literary pretensions, Mrs. Peterkin replied that she had no talent, that even her letters were "no more than telegrams." He persisted, however; and each time she came for a piano lesson he required her to bring a new sketch—much to the concern of Mrs. Bellamann, who begged her not to upset her husband with such shocking tales.

Then Carl Sandburg entered the picture. While in South Carolina to lecture before the Charleston Poetry Society, he visited Bellamann, an old friend; and the two men visited Lang Syne to pay their respects to Mrs. Peterkin. After an evening of music, during which Sandburg and one of Mrs. Peterkin's black employees "traded songs," the famous poet asked to see some of the sketches. After demurring, Mrs. Peterkin finally complied with the request; and Sandburg suggested that she submit her work for publication. Mrs. Peterkin shrewdly observed that the poet was, after all, her guest and therefore obliged to be complimentary; and she asked for the name of the best critic in America, someone who might render a more impartial judgment. Sandburg suggested H. L. Mencken; and Mrs. Peterkin promptly sent samples of her work to the Old Curmudgeon. He was so delighted with them that he accepted one for his own magazine, *Smart Set*, and recommended Mrs. Peterkin to

Emily Clark, a young woman in Richmond who was interested in promoting the cause of Southern letters.

Miss Clark, who had just begun publishing a magazine, *The Reviewer*, immediately wrote to Mrs. Peterkin and solicited some material. The reply, dated July 15, 1921, was characteristic: "I thank you for your kind letter. I shall be glad to send you something, but my things are crude, really stark plantation sketches. I think you will not want them. However, I'll send them with pleasure, and you can use your own judgment."[6]

After sending several sketches, Mrs. Peterkin realized that she had failed to enclose a stamped envelope for the inevitable return of the material; and in July she wrote again, including return postage and money for a subscription to the magazine. The manuscript, however, was not returned; nor was any of the subsequent material that she submitted. All in all, fourteen issues of *The Reviewer* contained some of Mrs. Peterkin's "crude, really stark plantation sketches"; and, while the response from the readership was not always favorable,[7] she received some warm words of praise from such well-known figures as James Branch Cabell and Joel Spingarn.

III   *First Fruits*: The Reviewer *and* Green Thursday

The Reviewer years provided Mrs. Peterkin with a valuable apprenticeship when she was allowed, through the grace of Miss Clark, to develop at her own pace without the discouragement of harsh editing and frequent rejections. For a woman of her temperament, it was perhaps the only way. One suspects that had she experienced the heartaches characteristic of most early literary careers, she would have quit the game and returned to her clubs and horticulture.

Because of the national interest generated by *The Reviewer* and perhaps because Mrs. Peterkin had enthusiastic and influential admirers, she was approached by Harcourt, Brace and Company and later by Alfred A. Knopf to publish a book about her plantation blacks. Mr. Alfred Harcourt advised her to take the series of *Reviewer* pieces, written at random, and to "weave it into a connected thing"[8]—words which frustrated and perplexed her. She sought advice from her more experienced friends (Sandburg, Mencken, Harriet Monroe, and Spingarn); and, while several expressed doubts that such a radical grafting was possible, they nevertheless told her to make the attempt. The result was *Green Thursday*, a collection of twelve sketches and stories involving Killdee, Rose, Missie, and Maum Hannah—a black family whose struggles with the land, the elements, and their individual consciences provide the subject matter for what can best be described as a loose plot highlighted by moments of primitive power and marred by inconsistencies and redundance.

Though Mrs. Peterkin was undoubtedly influenced by the editors of Harcourt, Brace, she eventually chose Alfred A. Knopf as her publisher, possibly because of Mencken's association with that firm. The book, released on September 12, 1924, was 192 pages and the initial printing was two thousand copies. Though its author was relatively unknown, and though the volume was finally published as a collection of short stories, it sold more than five thousand copies[9]—a tribute to Mrs. Peterkin's remarkable talent and perhaps to the influence of her small band of admirers.

IV   Consequences

After the publication of *Green Thursday*, Mrs. Peterkin had to worry for the first time about the widespread reaction of fellow South Carolinians. As long as her sketches were appearing in the "little magazines," there was small danger that the community at large would take notice of her budding literary career. *The Reviewer*, where all but one of her prose pieces had appeared, had a very limited circulation; and its readership was for the most part sophisticated enough to judge a writer on relevant grounds. The publication of a book, however, broadened considerably Mrs. Peterkin's audience; and the result was a certain amount of criticism from the "home folks."

Shortly after the volume appeared, she began to anticipate trouble and wrote to Emily Clark: "*Green Thursday* looks very beautiful to me, of course. . . I fear my own South Carolina audience will not be sympathetic. *The State*, the leading newspaper, edited by Mr. Gonzales, who himself has written several very charming Negro books, has been very careful to ignore me so far."[10]

Mrs. Peterkin's fears about her Southern audience's reaction were soon realized. For a while she was the target of considerable abuse, not only from local celebrants of the "genteel tradition" but also from close friends and from members of her family who feared that she would bring social ostracism to the whole clan. In a letter to Joel E. Spingarn, she discussed the problem: "My nearest of kin and my natural protectors think (they say) that to publish my raw crude things in *The Crisis* [the N.A.A.C.P. magazine] will win me the scorn of both black and white. That sounds bad. I'm not sure I could bear it . . . . The negroes say 'A cowardly man don' tote no broke bones . . . .' In time I shall achieve courage. I shall. Courage to face every aunt, uncle, cousin. But now, somehow, since they talked to me, I'm low-spirited. Down-hearted. My self-respect is at a pretty low ebb."[11]

Aside from the fact that Killdee, Rose, and Missie are not the familiar stereotypes beloved by readers of Thomas Nelson Page, there is very little in *Green Thursday* to offend Old South apologists. "Ashes," the only story which treats the white-black relationship, merely reconfirms the existence of *noblesse oblige* in post-bellum Southern society; and this concept, according to its most sympathetic interpreters, was the informing principle of the old plantation system. The rest of the stories deal with blacks in a pristine state and could not be construed as racial commentary except by the subtlest of critics. In 1924, Mrs. Peterkin's South Carolina critics were anything but subtle.

Proprieties other than racial ones were, however, at stake; and most of the criticism stemmed from a consideration of these. For one thing, Mrs. Peterkin was socially prominent—daughter of a well-known doctor, wife of a plantation owner, mother of a young son and heir—and for this reason she had a certain dignity to maintain, as well as responsibilities to perform. For such a woman to forsake kitchen and drawing room for the writing of fiction was, to some people, a disgrace in the South Carolina of the 1920's, particularly if she became the subject of news stories. Mrs. Peterkin's grandmother summarized polite opinion when she said, "no lady's name ever appears in a newspaper." At least one friend told Julia she'd "lose her social standing" if she achieved any more notoriety. In effect, it was "trashy" to be controversial, particularly if one were a woman.

Then too, by the standards of the time, her subject matter was anything but respectable. Arson, adultery, disfigurement, death—all these she presents in graphic detail; for she never avoided the sordidness of her fictional world. It would have been all right for a woman to join the Charleston Poetry Society (as Mrs. Peterkin did in 1925) and write sonnets about the Magnolia Gardens or the firing on Fort Sumter, but to deal so realistically with the sordid lives of

croppers, black or white, was something else again. Even her
father, a worldly man of science, lamented because she would not
write "more ladylike" stories; and in a letter one man speculated
that she would "soon be writing romances about mules." Mrs.
Peterkin replied, "I should love to, but I don't think I know enough
about mules."[12] In her next book, however, perhaps for spite, she
devoted a whole chapter to a mule named "Julia."

Finally, because of her coolly critical view of Fundamentalist
Puritanism in the black church, she incurred the disfavor of the
pietistic; and there were those who feared for her soul. One minister
presented himself at Lang Syne in order to bring about her salvation; and, when she told him that she felt in good spiritual health, he
replied: "Your books don't indicate it." He broke into fervent
prayer, calling upon the Lord to "open this woman's eyes and show
her that Satan is guiding her."[13]

According to her own accounts, she handled the situation with
poise and good humor, but the attacks stung her, as a letter to Emily
Clark indicates: "In this part of the world my book has not met with
much sympathy, but that does not surprise me at all. I said things
that no nice South Carolina lady ever says, and so I must be disciplined a bit even by my friends. . . . What I have done has given
me a lot of fun just in the doing, and that is compensation enough
besides the joy of having some real critics to encourage me to go
on."[14]

Those "real critics" were people like Carl Sandburg, who wrote
her: "It's a real and fine book. Some of it goes along just like you
talk; and so it is honestly personal. And again it's touched with the
overtones a book ought to have and that don't always go with
talk. . . . I was glad to be mentioned on the jacket as having even
slightly helped toward such a book."[15] And Joel Spingarn wrote that
"[n]othing so stark, taut, poignant, has come out of the South in fifty
years."[16]

These men, of course, were her early supporters; and their reaction was predictable; but in addition to them, such important literary organs as the *New York Times* were also highly complimentary:
"Mrs. Peterkin has shown herself in *Green Thursday* as a literary
artist without any prejudice except the saving artistic predilection
for unity and coherent form. Into the mold of the graceful form she
has chosen she pours the distillation of a rich, human observation of
the secret life of a people who have not yet been understood by the

whites, because the whites have always found it easier to laugh at it than to attempt to comprehend it."[17]

There were also favorable reviews in *Time, The Saturday Review of Literature* (H. S. Canby), *International Book Review* (Dora Mulkin), the *New York Herald Tribune* (Margery Latimer), the *Chicago Evening Post* (Frank H. Pettee), the *Richmond Times Dispatch* (Hunter Stagg), the *New York World* (Laurence Stallings), and the *Columbia Record* (Henry Bellamann). *The State*, however, ignored the book entirely; and Mrs. Peterkin attributed the snub to the jealousy of editor Ambrose Gonzalez, though there is no hard evidence that such was the motive.

Of particular interest is the response of blacks to the book. *Crisis,* the official organ of the National Association for the Advancement of Colored People, was particularly enthusiastic; and such approval was all the more significant because the words of praise were, according to *Crisis* editor James W. Ivy, written by W.E.B. DuBois himself.[18] The reviewer called *Green Thursday* a "beautiful book" and said of Mrs. Peterkin, "She is a Southern white woman but she has the eye and ear to see beauty and to know truth."[19]

Walter White was also pleased with the book and authorized a favorable review which appeared in over two hundred black newspapers nationwide. Mrs. Peterkin was delighted with such response and wrote to Emily Clark: "The Society for the Advancement of Colored People has given me a long and really discriminating review and they write they are sending out three hundred copies to papers. That pleases me, for I am glad to have approval from negroes themselves, and these down here cannot read much."[20] And to Spingarn she wrote:

It delighted me to have a kind word from Walter White. When I found the very people on whom I had counted on for sympathy here in reading my book all upset and indignant with me, not even indifferent but quite angry, then I thought "The negroes may hate me too!" But they seem to understand my intention better than the whites in many cases. This pleases me greatly. I had no intention of doing anything that could be construed as propaganda. I wanted to record my impressions of people who seemed interesting to me. Doing it gave me much pleasure, and I felt that I was quite within my rights in spending my time so. Others differ with me.[21]

In the response to *Green Thursday*, there are at least two significant factors. First, it is interesting to note Mrs. Peterkin's bitterness toward the people in her own state. It sprang not merely from what she considered to be the studied silence of *The State* but also from a number of personal indignities which she had to suffer from members of her own race and class. And this bitterness, born of keen disappointment, was to remain with her for the rest of her life. Shortly before her death when she was asked at a dinner what her friends and neighbors thought of her literary career, she leaned forward and whispered, "They hated me."[22]

Second, the attitude of the blacks throughout the country was, during the 1920's, warm and sympathetic. They undoubtedly recognized Mrs. Peterkin to be an honest writer who avoided the demeaning stereotypes popular on Broadway as well as in Atlanta. Whatever Mrs. Peterkin was, she was not abusive or condescending; to the blacks of America of the 1920's—when the new Ku Klux Klan was at the height of its political ascendence and when black-faced singer Al Jolson was called "the World's Greatest Entertainer"—the quiet sympathy of the South Carolina woman must have been reassuring.

V Black April

Always modest in her literary pretensions, Mrs. Peterkin at first seemed to doubt that she could manage a full-blown novel. In 1923, she wrote somewhat wistfully to Emily Clark, "There's a wonderful novel waiting here at Lang Syne for somebody to write,"[23] and she suggested that Joseph Hergesheimer, whose work she admired, might be the one to write it. Several years later, however, after the critical success of *Green Thursday*, she began to realize something of her own capabilities and decided to essay the task herself. Carl Sandburg encouraged her, but added a warning: "Go slow and sure with another book."[24] She took the advice; and it was three years before the publication of *Black April*, a book which brought her before the national reading public and which opened the door to the even greater success that followed.

As in the earlier sketches and stories, she adhered closely in this book to her own experience; she was still unwilling to wander far from the bounds of Lang Syne plantation. As she herself said:

Black April goes by the name of a novel, but a large part of it is fact. I got the habit of utilizing incident when I wrote *Green Thursday*. I had written those sketches as the facts on which they are based had crystallized in my consciousness and had to be given form. In *Black April* incidents are blended together, of course, in the hope of achieving continuity. When you are writing out of your experience you don't have to rely to any great extent upon your imagination. I have lived among the negroes. I like them. They are my friends, and I have learned so much from them. The years on the plantation have given me plenty of material, my life has been rich, so why try to improve upon the truth?[25]

The story she chose from her experience was that of the foreman whose terrible ordeal had first driven her to Dr. Bellamann. Yet she was either naive or shrewd when she suggested that she had not attempted to improve on reality. A comparison between *Black April* and her earlier treatment of the incident in *The Reviewer* suggests just how much she had learned in her years of apprenticeship. While some structural difficulties appear in the novel (see Chapter Three for a detailed discussion), her "blending of incidents" lifts the episode to new heights and informs it with a thematic complexity that approaches the highest literary sophistication.

VI *A Switch and Critical Acclaim*

Apparently unhappy with the pessimistic outlook that Knopf held about the sales potential of her work, Mrs. Peterkin assigned the publication of *Black April* to Bobbs-Merrill, much to the annoyance of Mencken, who had promoted the original association. Her new publishers heralded the book with an extensive advertising campaign, and the results were more than gratifying to Mrs. Peterkin, as evidenced in a letter to Anne Johnstone: "Mr. Knopf had convinced me that my stuff would never sell: that to advertise it would be a foolish waste of money. I was bitterly discouraged. You've no idea how much so. Now, I walk on air! Let the S.C. ladies gnash their teeth as much as they like! Let the heathen rage! Somebody *does* believe in me!"[26]

Once again, as the early reactions to her novel began to surface, Mrs. Peterkin was worried about the reaction of South Carolinians. As she wrote to D.L. Chambers at Bobbs-Merrill, "Here a woman must write with sentimentality and stiltedness to write according to the S.C. code of good taste."[27] Interestingly enough, other Southern writers, male as well as female, were experiencing this same reaction. The Fugitive Group at Vanderbilt University complained about the "moonlight-and-magnolias" school of Southern literature,

and in the initial issue of their now-famous magazine John Crowe
Ransom wrote: "The Fugitive flees from nothing so quickly as the
high-caste Brahmins of the old South."[28]

Perhaps because of a sympathetic understanding of Mrs. Peterkin's problems in writing such a book as *Black April*, Donald Davidson, then literary editor for the *Nashville Tennessean*, wrote a glowing review of the book which typified the reaction of the more
enlightened Southern men of letters. He summarized his evaluation
as follows:

Yes, April is "man-size," and so is the book. It is powerful, serene, good-
humored, tempestuous by turns, with all the primitive passions kept for so
many years in their undisturbed original state. The folklorist may read this
book, if he wishes, for its infinite store of superstitions and sayings; the
sociologist may read it for its account of a definite social group which has
maintained itself practically untouched by civilization; everybody else may
read the book for what it is, perhaps the first genuine novel in English of the
Negro as a human being.[29]

And Davidson was not alone among Southerners in his enthusiasm. Stark Young wrote to her and, after discussing *Green
Thursday*, said: "But of course *Black April* goes much further—how
much further—as it should—more scope, more canvass, variety,
power, thread. I believe absolutely in your gift, of life and of art."[30]
Julian Harris, the son of Joel Chandler Harris, wrote in the Columbus (Georgia) *Enquirer-Sun* that Mrs. Peterkin deserved the
Pulitzer Prize. And *The State* broke its silence; it not only published
flattering reviews but stated in a generous editorial, which should
have wiped away any past bitterness, that "[i]t is one of the most
enduring stories, we think, of those who have been fashioned by the
whites out of the dark material, the flesh and blood of these jungle-
folk held and estranged. . . . "[31]

Mrs. Peterkin was so elated that she wrote to Chambers about the
phenomenon of local acceptance: "the old state is coming my way. I
see signs. The best are already alongside. The rest wavering. I may
be nominated for Congress or something fine yet. Have already
been invited to run for State President of Federation of Women's
Clubs!"[32] And there were other honors, some of them dubious ones.
She was invited to speak throughout the region. Curiosity seekers
drove down to Fort Motte on Sundays to catch a glimpse of her,
much to her annoyance. And, in a state which often seems to be

inhabited by one large family, distant relatives began to make their existence known; they were suddenly aware of long-overlooked kinships. But, as the crown of her local honors, she received an honorary degree from her alma mater, Converse College. She had been forgiven her sins, real or imagined.

Outside the South, the reaction to *Black April* was equally gratifying. Charles Puckette in *The Saturday Review of Literature* wrote: "In many respects this, Mrs. Peterkin's second published volume of fiction dealing with negroes in the South, must stand as the most genuinely successful attempt yet made to capture the soul of these people. This book is put down with the feeling that one stands nearer to truth than one has stood before, in a field of fiction the surface of which has been often scratched and the rich depths seldom upturned. . . . Other fiction of negro life seems false in the light of Mrs. Peterkin's achievement."[33]

Robert Herrick of *The New Republic* said approximately the same thing: "possibly the most convincing presentation that has yet been made by a white person." He also called the book "a considerable work of art," and he praised its "mastery of dialect."[34] He was disturbed by her "too abundant use of superstition," which he felt revealed her white Southern point of view; but he admitted that it was "almost impossible to tell whether the writer was an alien observer or a Negro become wholly conscious and expressive."

The opinions expressed in both *The Saturday Review* and *The New Republic* are significant since they represent the contemporary thinking of elements generally hostile to the South and to its racial attitudes. Later self-styled Liberals would look back on Mrs. Peterkin with ahistorical eyes and see her as another in a series of Southern apologists who were infected with the disease of prejudice (see Chapter Seven); but, to those who called themselves Liberals in the 1920's and early 1930's, she was in the vanguard of Southern "progressivism."

There were, of course, critics who did not find the book as rewarding as those cited above. For example, John W. Crawford in the *New York Times* found the handling of the dialect less satisfying than in the work of Gonzales; and he also felt that Mrs. Peterkin had invested her characters with "an ill-advised sensibility."[35] Others, while generally praising the novel, found fault with its structure (too much irrelevant detail) or with the prose (too choppy). But, all in all, *Black April* was a critical and financial success.

Fortified with the knowledge that she was appreciated both by South Carolinians and by the nation at large, Mrs. Peterkin immediately made plans to begin a new novel. For one thing, she felt that she had omitted many details of plantation life that demanded recording. Moreover, another character needed additional definition—a black woman of remarkable vitality and independence whom she had treated only superficially in a *Reviewer* sketch. With these ends in mind, she spent the summer of 1927 at the Mac-Dowell Colony in Peterborough, New Hampshire, and began the novel *Scarlet Sister Mary.*

The MacDowell Colony was a community that provided writers with the two things most conducive to creative productivity: solitude in which to work and the company of kindred spirits who could provide criticism and advice. Membership was by invitation only, and it is some indication of Mrs. Peterkin's success that she was among "the elect" although she probably entered into the experiment with some reluctance. Earlier she had written to Emily Clark: "As a rule I loathe people who like myself are trying to write, so I avoid them, along with their clubs. This sounds ugly. It is so, however. . . . "[36] In view of such an opinion, she was perversely pleased that Mrs. MacDowell was ill during her stay at Peterborough; for the evening social activities (command performances) at the home of the hostess were eliminated. She did, however, enjoy the time spent with fellow South Carolinian DuBose Heyward, the highly acclaimed author of *Porgy,* and wrote to Chambers: "Dubose Heyward is here and I adore him. He's my chief defender in S.C., bless him."[37]

Apparently she made remarkable progress on her novel during this period, which lasted until late August; for, despite the interruption of guests after she returned to Lang Syne, she finished *Scarlet Sister Mary* in less than a year; and it was published in the fall of 1928.

VII   Scarlet Sister Mary

The chief virtue of *Scarlet Sister Mary,* aside from its careful craftsmanship, is the portrayal of the main character—as spirited a heroine as almost any in modern American literature. As Mrs. Peterkin depicts her she is the embodiment of joie de vivre, an earthy woman who takes her pleasure where she can find it, rejoices in giving life to her nine children (eight illegitimate), and embodies to a fault the Christian virtues of charity and kindness.

These qualities, rendered in a well-structured action, made Mary Mrs. Peterkin's own favorite among her many characters. And the affections of the authoress were shared by most of the reviewers who were, if anything, more enthusiastic about *Scarlet Sister Mary* than they were about *Black April*. This time *The State* ran a complimentary review even before the publication date. Herschel Brickell, writing in *The Saturday Review of Literature*, said that the book "firmly establishes its author as an interpreter of Negro character, but more than that, it leaves no room for doubt that she is a novelist whose work has enduring quality."[38] Robert Herrick was once again complimentary in *The New Republic*; he wrote that *Scarlet Sister Mary* was "something more than a novel—the revelation of a race, which has lived with the whites for hundreds of years, without becoming known beneath the skin."[39]

Ben Wasson, in *Outlook and Independent*, recognized Mrs. Peterkin's departure from the use of stereotypes, often the resort of less significant portrayers of black life: "Mrs. Peterkin escapes such things; she is above them. Her book is real because she realizes that people, be they black or white, are fundamentally alike."[40] Joseph Warren Beach, in his excellent and significant study *The Twentieth Century Novel*, agreed; he found the novel "entirely free from any flavoring of patronage, sentimentality, apology, defense."[41] Another well-known portrayer of black life, Roark Bradford, wrote in a letter that *Scarlet Sister Mary* was even finer than *Black April*, a novel he had regarded as nearly perfect.[42]

Such reviews naturally boosted sales, and the novel very quickly became a best seller. The fact that it was banned in Boston no doubt increased the demand for it, but it was probably not just Mary's joie de vivre which offended the censor. At this particular time, Mencken, whose support was not always an unmixed blessing, was having a feud with the Reverend Frank T. Chase and his Watch and Ward Society (whose self-appointed task was to purge the newsstands and bookstores of all "immoral" literature). Mencken's *American Mercury* had offended the Reverend Mr. Chase; as a result, the magazine had been "proscribed"; and the Sage of Baltimore, in a characteristic gesture, had rushed to Boston, deliberately courted arrest, and then contested the case in the courts. As in the instance of the Scopes trial, Mencken's flamboyance and studied arrogance solidified the opposition against him; and the result was a ban which affected not only the *American Mercury* and *Scarlet Sister Mary* but also the works of Theodore Dreiser, Upton Sinclair, Jim Tully, Lion

Feuchtwanger, and Bertrand Russell.[43] The ensuing national publicity, however, probably resulted in a net gain in sales of the books of all these authors.

In 1929, Mrs. Peterkin found herself the subject of a major literary controversy; and, while the outcome was gratifying and profitable to her, the furor must have caused her some pain and embarrassment. The difficulty arose as the result of a decision by the Pulitzer advisory committee, in April of 1928, to change the qualifications for the prize-winning novel. Originally, the award was presented to the work of fiction which "shall best present the wholesome atmosphere of American life and the highest standards of American manners and manhood." In order to widen the possibilities for the selection board, the clause was altered to read, "preferably one which shall best present the whole atmosphere of American life." Perhaps the change was made to allow consideration to those works which were critical of national life and manners, but another factor was surely at work. The Advisory Committee of the School of Journalism at Columbia University, empowered to make the final selection on all awards, had decided to reject the recommendation of the fiction award jury that the prize be given to John B. Oliver's *Victim and Victor*. As a result of this action, Dr. Richard S. Burton, chairman of the judges for the fiction award, resigned his position and requested that he not be asked to serve again. A month later the award was made to the fiction jury's second choice—*Scarlet Sister Mary* by Julia Peterkin.

Because of the committee's stated policy, Mrs. Peterkin, when told by someone that she might receive the award, expressed doubt that *Scarlet Sister Mary* would win.[44] But win it did; and, though Mencken wired her to refuse the award since the committee was "entirely devoid of critical talent or ability," Mrs. Peterkin, always mindful of her manners, replied that she would consider such a refusal impolite. On May 14, it was announced that all winners had been notified of their awards and that no one had declined.

On the day of the announcement, Bobbs-Merrill put five presses to work printing additional copies of the book, and eventually it sold over a million copies in all editions, both in English and in Spanish.[45] It was the first American novel to be published in a "featherweight airplane edition," the forerunner of the paperback;[46] and it made Mrs. Peterkin a national celebrity. As a result, she served with Ernest Boyd and Lewis Mumford on the board of judges for a ten thousand dollar novel contest, was chosen as a member of the editorial board of the Literary Guild of America, and was honored at a literary dinner in New York that was well attended by prominent writers and reviewers. She also began to enjoy the spoils which are always proffered to the famous and successful writer. The high-paying "slick" magazines began to publish her work, and in 1929 she published stories and articles in the *Ladies' Home Journal, The Saturday Evening Post,* and *Country Gentleman.*

VIII   Bright Skin

Mrs. Peterkin's third novel, *Bright Skin,* was published by Bobbs-Merrill in April, 1932, with an explanation on the dust jacket about the four barren years. Mrs. Peterkin, they said, had worked with added care on this book because she wished it to be a mature and polished work of art. Critics, however, were quick to indicate the deficiencies which suggested other reasons. John Chamberlain, writing in the *New York Times,* found the characters superficial and unconvincing: "One suspects that Mrs. Peterkin, for all her familiarity with the externals of these strange people, can never get at their insides. She has made them gay or drooping or disappointed puppets in an appealingly unusual setting. A member of another race can watch but cannot share their lives."[47] And Archer Winston in *The Bookman* raised another objection:

Mrs. Peterkin has written four volumes, but they are only one novel. She must now decide whether to start a new novel or add another volume to her already masterful creation of Negro life. In the latter case she must remember that her stage is fully set. The heroic figure of April begging to be buried "in a man-size box" though his legs have been amputated, and the marvelous ever-sinning Si' May'e lend to their stories a crowning quality which is lacking in *Bright Skin.* For in the end Cricket eludes us; she has gone where the author cannot follow, and her going confirms our suspicion that we have learned little that was not said in the earlier volumes.[48]

As these comments suggest, *Bright Skin* was not a critical success; and it marked the end of Mrs. Peterkin's career as a writer of fiction. Despite a few good reviews, she was probably discouraged by the critical reception the book received in quarters where her work had previously been praised; and perhaps she realized that she had exhausted her literary resources and could not break through the barrier of her own experience to create a fictional world of broader significance. From time to time, there was talk of another novel in progress; but, during later years, she told an interviewer that she had no unsolicited manuscripts. The new novel, if it ever existed, probably never took concrete form. Like Pindar, however, she still had some arrows left in her quiver; and she published one significant book of nonfiction after *Bright Skin*.

IX Roll, Jordan, Roll

In Mrs. Peterkin's last major work, *Roll, Jordan, Roll* (see Chapter Six), she abandons all pretense of overall unity and returns to the short portraits and anecdotes with which she began her literary career in *The Reviewer*. Indeed, a number of the pieces are slightly revised versions of those earlier sketches—modified, improved, but in essence the same material.

Mrs. Peterkin's stated aim in *Roll, Jordan, Roll* was to capture the plantation experience before it faded from the memory of modern society, and she defines explicitly many of her own social and historical views—ones which are either absent from the fictional works or only vaguely implicit. The book was a byproduct of an old friendship with Mrs. Doris Ullman, a photographer who shared Mrs. Peterkin's interest in the life of the Gullah; and Mrs. Ullman's dark, brooding plantation portraits serve as a visual gloss to Mrs. Peterkin's text.

In general, the reviews of *Roll, Jordan, Roll* were cautious but sympathetic. John Chamberlain in the *New York Times* criticized the author for tending to "generalize . . . solely from what she sees"; and he suggests that Walter White's *The Fire in the Flint* is a much more accurate description of the black experience. Chamberlain concludes that, within her limitations, Mrs. Peterkin is a valuable portrayer of "the brighter side of the picture."[49]

X The Final Years

After the publication in 1934 of a clothbound version of her *Country Gentleman* sketch, "A Plantation Christmas," Mrs. Peterkin turned her attentions to other than literary matters: to the management of Lang Syne; to Democratic party politics (to support the New Deal until 1940); and to her family, which by this time included a grandson, William Peterkin III. But ample evidence exists that she never completely renounced the world of letters. In 1936, she taught creative writing at Bennington, Vermont; and, in the fall of that year, she joined such distinguished literary figures as Ber-

nard DeVoto, John Mason Brown, and Robert Frost for a conference at Bread Loaf Inn where she lectured and evaluated the manuscripts of young writers. In 1937, she contributed her most significant critical article to the *North American Review;* and she stated
in unequivocal terms her belief in the new "Realism" to be found in
current literature about the black. In 1939, she agreed to meet with
a group of Southern writers in Savannah to discuss their common
problems, but she was prevented from doing so by the death of her
husband. And she occasionally attended literary functions at the
University of South Carolina or entertained writers like Jesse Stuart
at her Fort Motte home.

But her personal life became increasingly troubled, for sorrow
was a frequent visitor at Lang Syne plantation. In addition to William Peterkin's death (after years of illness), she also suffered the
suicide of her daugher-in-law and the loss of another good foreman.
Then, too, the Depression years were difficult ones for farmers; and,
because she was growing old, the responsibilities of plantation management weighed heavily on her shoulders. In 1941, for example,
persistent rainfall completely ruined the cotton crop; and she was
forced to forego a much-needed vacation in order to supervise the
planting of food crops to feed the blacks during the winter.[50] In
1954, she was troubled by drought, as well as by a series of plantation illnesses.

She was also depressed by the turmoil of the war years and wrote
to a friend, "the whole world seems all awry, wrong, upset."[51] And
later, "So many things have come my way these latter years that I
fear I'm becoming an apprehensive soul who needs to know that all
is well with those I prize."[52] And again, "The good God did a cruel
thing when he made human beings so they'd grow old and frail and
end life in pain. To be ill is so humiliating. Why couldn't we end like
apples on a tree? Ripen, become lively and fragrant, then when
perfect, drop easily without clinging to the bough."[53]

But, like the blacks she admired so much, she endured; she per-
formed her demanding role as chatelaine of Lang Syne, cared for
her family, and found occasional moments of happiness to commemorate in her rich and articulate letters. No ripe apple, she
wrinkled, grayed, and became a sick, troubled old woman; and only
her clear, blue eyes reminded others of the brilliant and beautiful
authoress who had, for a time, won the admiration of an entire
nation. Then, shortly before her eighty-first birthday, she surrendered to a final illness and died on August 10, 1961.

CHAPTER 2

The Drama of Man in Nature

MRS. Peterkin wrote to Emily Clark when *Green Thursday* was first proposed that "Harcourt and Brace want a book of mine, but want the thread of a novel to bind the sketches. They tell me Sinclair Lewis likes them, but says they are for 'a limited, sophisticated audience; simplified into a novel they'll reach a larger public.' I'm perplexed. What do you think? Carl Sandburg says No. I'm uncertain."[1]

Her perplexity is understandable, but a great deal of truth existed in the proposition that a novel would outsell a short story collection since such has always been the case. But what might have been desirable from the standpoint of economics was not necessarily advisable as fictional technique; and Lewis seems to have been preoccupied with considerations more appropriate to a sales executive than to a practicing novelist. His advice only served to confuse Mrs. Peterkin, who was always humble before experienced "professional" writers although her own literary instincts were usually more trustworthy than those of her several famous advisers. Certainly the central difficulty of *Green Thursday* can be laid at Lewis's doorstep, and it is barely possible that the book in its original form was a minor American classic.

The work is concerned with one Gullah Family, that of Killdee Pinesett, as its members attempt to scratch out a living from the land and to come to grips with the basic dangers, sorrows, and pleasures which are the lot of every human being. Included in Killdee's family are his wife, Rose; his aunt, Maum Hannah; his infant children; and later Missie, an adopted daughter. The first of the connected stories exclusively concerns Maum Hannah, but the later episodes all deal with the family in some form or another. Though each story may feature a different member, all deal in some significant way with their common destiny which includes such

archetypal experiences as falling in love, dying, struggling to survive, worrying about God, and quarreling with one another. And
yet—though some of the stories are outstanding examples of short
fiction—*Green Thursday* has significant structural weaknesses.

I *Structural Problems*

The structural problem is really twofold. In the first place, there
are difficulties inherent in any novel that is a "suite" of shorter
pieces. It is one thing to give unity to a group of stories by a common
setting (as in James Joyce's *Dubliners*) or even with characters who
appear in more than one segment (Sherwood Anderson's *Wines-
burg, Ohio*), but it is quite another thing to make each separate and
complete action function in a "continuing action" that itself has a
beginning, middle, and end.[2]

If a short story is to embody significant literary values, it must
have its own movement—some revelation or "epiphany" which is
meaningful to a character or to the reader. Yet, for the movement in
each of the twelve stories to meld perfectly into a larger, coherent
pattern of movement, there would have to be some continued development of theme or character from segment to segment, and, at
the same time an ending for each story that is sufficiently resolved to
be esthetically satisfying. So even theoretically the problem of structure in such a work is a formidable one, and Mr. Lewis was using the
language carelessly when he suggested that the sketches could be
"simplified" into a novel. The project he suggested was—technically
speaking—about as simple as juggling twelve pie plates in such a
way that they form a perfect parabola.

But, practically speaking, Mrs. Peterkin's problem was all the
more impossible because she had already written her collection of
shorter pieces; and to suggest that she tie them together ex post
facto with "the thread of a novel" (an imprecise phrase) was to ask
her to perform radical surgery on twelve separate living organisms
and then to sew them together again so that they all functioned as
part of one vital body.

Unfortunately, there is no record of the emendations that Mrs.
Peterkin made at this point; but, in comparing the printed version
with the *Reviewer* sketches, one can see that names were changed,
incidents added or subtracted, and smaller unities were sacrificed to
the lean prospect of achieving a larger one. Some of this mischief is
evident in the individual stories; yet, surprisingly enough, a few

survived as unified works of art. That they did so is no tribute to
Sinclair Lewis or to Alfred Harcourt of Harcourt, Brace. On the
other hand, even friends shared in the blame. Both Carl Sandburg
and Harriet Monroe, after saying that Lewis's suggestion was impossible, encouraged her to try to fulfill it in order to publish the
book. She tried; and a comparison of the earlier sketches with the
published book reveals significant alterations designed to give the
narrative an overall unity. Then she broke with Harcourt, Brace and
took the manuscript to Alfred A. Knopf, Inc., which published
Green Thursday in 1924 as a group of short stories and sketches; as a
result, the economic advantages of the novel were ultimately sacrificed anyway.

II *Prologue*

Green Thursday begins with a description of the plantation and
surrounding countryside that seems at first glance to be merely the
definition of setting.[3] The author depicts the woods, fields, and
pastures that sprawl along the red clay hilltops, the twin yellow-
brown rivers that flow for miles on either side of the rich farmland
and meet to form a single stream, and the hazy blue hills that line
the distant horizon. These introductory paragraphs, as skillfully constructed as any in the later works, serve not only to delineate the
physical backdrop for all the stories in the volume, but also to define
in a sense the limitations of Mrs. Peterkin's literary concern. The
remoteness of the scene—its isolation from the complex, urban society of twentieth-century America—makes it possible for her to
examine the archetypal experiences in Gullah life (love, birth,
death) without reference to the political and social controversy that
has surrounded the status of the blacks in the South since the advent
of slavery. As she told Emily Clark, "I mean to present these people
in a patient struggle with fate, and not in any race conflict at all."[4]
     Thus the hills—"the outside world"—serve merely as a backdrop
for the immediate natural setting and are too distant to be seen as
anything more distinct than a "low line of faint blue." Neither they
nor the outer world they represent can be said to play an active role
in the action. Only nature, as viewed and interpreted by the black,
is relevant as an external motivating force. The river, the swamp,
the cotton fields—the elements—function actively in shaping the
action of the stories; but it is as if this action were set in a land as

exotic, yet as specifically defined, as Joseph Conrad's Belgian Congo. Except for Mrs. Peterkin's occasional references to such modern inventions as the automobile, these twelve stories might have taken place in the nineteenth or the eighteenth century; and the sense of specific locality is established, for the most part, through natural description and the speech of the characters— details which only a botanist or a linguistic historian could localize with any certainty.

But there is still more here than merely definition and limitation. In reading Mrs. Peterkin's description, the perceptive reader is soon aware that many of the details function on a higher level. For, in the subsequent paragraph in which she describes the flood season, the author is using the ancient symbolic meaning of the river to show the plantation's invulnerability to the currents of time and change. The two rivers "lunge and tear at the hillsides that hold the plantation above them"; then they return, defeated, to their "rightful channels"; but the plantation "sits always calm. Undisturbed. The rivers can never reach it." And then—more explicitly—"the outside world may wamble and change, but it cannot come any nearer."

In such a timeless world, then, Mrs. Peterkin's blacks plow behind slow mules, huddle over uncertain fires, or hunt for food and adventure in the swamp. The old archetypal life-struggle is presented in most of its manifestations—tilling of the earth, hunting the land, the battle with nature's cyclic forces. "There is nothing," she writes, "to hint that life here could be sweet or that its current runs free and strong. Winter, summer, birth, death, these seem to be all." And so the scene is removed from time—the rivers of change which rush on either side; and the simple details of Gullah life are symbolically transformed into the eternal drama of man in nature.

Then, in the final section of her introductory description, Mrs. Peterkin provides her readers with an image which presumes a great deal for itself and invites (rather than demands) a mythological interpretation of much of the action that follows:

Right where the two roads meet is a sycamore tree. Its milk-white branches reach up to the sky. Its pale, silken leaves glisten and whisper incomplete cadences in the hot summer sunshine.

When frost crisps the leaves and stains them and cuts them away, they flutter down, leaving golden balls to adorn every bough.

There is hardly a sign of the black twisted roots. There is not a trace to be seen of their silent, tense struggle as they grope deep down in the earth. There is nothing to show how they reach and grapple and hold, or how in the darkness down among the worms they work out mysterious chemistries that change damp clay into beauty.[5]

The careful development of this image for three paragraphs—the last in the opening section—is sufficient evidence of its import and clarifies its essential meaning. The sycamore tree is the tree of life (Genesis iii, 22; Revelation xxii, 2) that reaches toward heaven yet is rooted in the clay-deep earth. Both the aspirations and the struggles of human existence are embodied in the image, but aspiration derives its sustenance from struggle. The reader is, in effect, brought to the gate of the primal garden by the implications of the symbol—man, halfway between heaven and earth, is caught in a struggle between divine aspirations and animal needs.

The central conflict of the book is thus defined, carefully yet with the seeming casualness of a Picasso print. Killdee and Rose are, to some extent, Adam and Eve; and their fall is the fall of mankind— the oldest of all the Judaeo-Christian myths restated once again within the framework of a specific action. Mrs. Peterkin does not, however, follow the myth so closely that it controls or completely informs the narrative. Like William Faulkner, she may use myth to give dimension to her story; but, since she is never possessed by it, many significant elements in *Green Thursday* have nothing to do with the Genesis story.

Aside from its primary symbolic meaning, the sycamore tree divides the world of black and white. One road runs to the Big House of the white owner, and the other goes to the quarters where the blacks live. The first road "bends with a swift, smooth curve and glides into a grove of cedars and live oaks and magnolias"; obviously, this road is the easier one and leads gently to a world of beauty. The second road, a "straggling rain-rutted fork runs along the edge of a field to a cluster of weather-beaten houses." The meaning of the contrast is obvious. The road of the white man is easier, pleasanter, more comfortable. The road of the black is a more difficult one that leads to poverty and hardship. The sycamore tree unites the two roads, standing as it does at the meeting point; and thus they are two forks of the road of life. It is down that straggling rain-rutted fork that Julia Peterkin chooses to take her reader.

III *"Ashes"—Maum Hannah*

The first story, "Ashes," which introduces Killdee and Rose only in a passing reference, is concerned with the plight of Maum Hannah, an ancient black woman who is threatened with eviction from her rickety, weatherbeaten cabin by a white man who wishes to occupy the property. When the man first arrives to survey the scene, he gives her a coin as a sop to his conscience; Maum Hannah realizes the seriousness of her plight; for, as she tells her cat, the man is "po-buckra." This term of course, is not so much a commentary on the man's financial resources as on his background and character. For, to the class-conscious black community, "po-buckra" are people with no sense of propriety. Traditionally, they have neither the intelligence nor the manners to respect the dignity of the blacks; and, when times became difficult, they frequently adopted the role of enemy or exploiter.

The night that Maum Hannah is told to leave, she sits by the clay hearth and smokes her pipe until dawn, worrying over the future. Unwilling to impose on her nephew Killdee or to endure the sharp tongue of Rose, the old woman thinks longingly of the grave. Then, because she is among "the saved," she prays to Jesus for deliverance. In this speech and in the ensuing action, Mrs. Peterkin emphasizes not only the intensity of the black's faith but also its simplicity. Maum Hannah asks for a sign, invoking Christ's supernatural grace. At that moment, in the heat of her fervor, her arms tremble and jerk, and ashes from her pipe spill onto the floor. Possessed of perfect trust, she believes she has been given her sign. She rises and looks out the front door, only to find in nature—a frequent source of revelation to the Gullah—further evidence of God's intent: the eastern sky is a fiery red.

Thanking Jesus for His guidance, she takes a flaming brand from her fireplace and burns down the white man's house. Then, in obedience to the law, she walks into town to confess. Upon inquiry, she learns that the sheriff lives in a white-columned house on the top of the hill—an indication that he is a man of some means; but the reader soon finds out that he is something more. As the old woman stumbles through her confession, the sheriff's attitude changes from one of paternal amusement to profound sympathy. As he stares at her wrinkled face and nervous hands, he is, in fact, moved to tears. He takes her into the kitchen, orders breakfast for her, and then warns her not to tell anyone else what she has just confessed to him. He is tacitly promising, of course, that he will not tell anyone either. In contrast to the "po-buckra," he is a gentleman and possesses a sense of noblesse oblige.

Though the story has some virtues—among them vivid descriptive passages and authenticity of dialect—it is, in the final analysis, a failure that is certainly the least satisfying selection in the volume. Its weaknesses are manifold, but the most significant is the author's inability or unwillingness to create credible characters. Not only do they fail to convince the reader of their essential humanity, but they also fail as stereotypes. Stereotyped sheriffs do not live in plantation houses and dispense grace with breakfast.

IV *Killdee and Rose and Missie*

"Green Thursday," from which the volume takes its name, provides an interesting contrast to "Ashes" as well as a more satisfactory introduction to Killdee and Rose, the central characters in the remaining stories. While "Ashes" is concerned with the relationship between black and white, "Green Thursday" is concerned with the relationship between man and God. Moreover, while Maum Hannah and the sheriff are imperfect stereotypes who perform roles in a drama where character is subordinate to plot and theme, Rose and Killdee are credible human beings caught up in ancient struggles with the land and with the dictates of conscience.

The story is told through the eyes of Killdee who, as the scene opens, is plowing his fields on Green Thursday (Ascension Day) in defiance of a taboo against such activity. The morning is clear and bright with sunshine; but Killdee, despite his masculine pragmatism and his contempt for superstition, cannot entirely forget the warnings he has heard as a child that lightning will strike the fields of blasphemers and punish with fire those who do not respect the holy day. Against the vague guilt that he feels, Killdee measures the urgent necessity of plowing the weeds before they choke the young plants.

What religion forbids, nature demands—and this irreconcilable dilemma is the major theme in *Green Thursday* as well as in *Scarlet Sister Mary*. It is of a primal nature with implications that go to the heart of the Christian ethic, and Mrs. Peterkin develops these implications with a fine impartiality that reveals her early allegiance to the scientific vision. Killdee is the natural man imperfectly conditioned to live in a society dominated by a Puritan Fundamentalism. His tragedy is that he can neither follow his natural inclinations without remorse nor submit to the discipline of a doctrine he cannot respect. And so he wavers between defiance and fear.

Suddenly, as Killdee daydreams of his daughter and an expected second child, dark clouds begin to gather; and, before he can reach home, thunder and lightning fill the sky. For a moment he speculates about the possibility of lightning striking the cabin and dismisses the idea from his head. After putting the mule in the barn—since all good farmers take care of the animals first—he goes inside to see about his family. Rose berates him for violating the Green Thursday taboo, and they argue about his alleged blasphemy and about the difficulty of Rose's confinement which makes it impossible for her to help in the fields or to care for the child adequately. Already there is trouble in paradise; and the lightning and thunder, which frighten Rose to distraction, serve not only to motivate the argument between them but also to objectify it—an instance among many where Mrs. Peterkin uses her setting as more than a mere backdrop.

Then the first in a series of misfortunes occurs. Killdee hears ominous noises in the stable and rushes out to find the mule lying in the dirt, its belly swollen with "colic." Killdee cries for Rose to bring the kerosene (a folk remedy), for he recognizes that the animal's condition is dangerous and possibly fatal. The mule is, of course, as vital to their existence as the land itself; and Killdee immediately wonders if he and the mule are not being punished for plowing on Green Thursday. When the mule gets to its feet, however, Killdee talks himself out of his fears; he blames the near-tragedy on the mule's bad teeth and on a diet of rotten corn. The natural explanation triumphs momentarily over the supernatural, but the possibility of divine retribution enters Killdee's head.

Then, in a climax that strains the credibility of chance to the breaking point, Rose, whom Killdee has sent to the house because she is afraid of lightning, comes screaming with the baby in her arms, its tiny body scorched by fire. The child has either been struck by lightning or has gone too near the fire. Rose, who has been crouching beneath the covers in fear of God's punishment, does not know what has happened; but the question is important. If the child has been struck by lightning, Killdee's presumption has been punished; if she has been burned by the fire, Rose's superstition, which sent her scurrying under the covers, is to blame.

Once again Mrs. Peterkin is offering the alternatives of natural and supernatural explanation, but she does so this time with more ambiguity than in "Ashes" where the intervention of the supernatural is a possibility only to Maum Hannah. Here everyone is in doubt—Rose, Killdee, and reader.

Immediately Killdee sends Rose to get Maum Hannah, whose homeopathic remedies serve the black community in lieu of a physician, but the old woman is unable to save Baby Rose. After the child has died, Rose becomes hysterical; and she denounces both God and Killdee. Bitterly, she blames her husband for the tragedy and says that he is the one who should suffer. Maum Hannah, whose faith is benign and mature, says that God has done what is right. Killdee looks out the door and sees only thick, black night.

Here the darkness functions as the oldest symbol of evil, in this case an evil which is all-pervasive, invading the firelit cabin from the heavens themselves; and Killdee begins to wrestle with the most perplexing of theological dilemmas—how a benevolent God can let the innocent suffer. But neither Killdee nor Mrs. Peterkin attempts to justify the ways of God to man. Killdee, after first ascribing the death to providential vengeance (admitting his own guilt), soon begins to blame Rose for her superstition and cowardice. In the final analysis, he returns to the possibility of his own guilt; but he does not forgive God for making the world as it is; and, in the end, he must admit his helplessness in the face of superior power. Like Satan in John Milton's *Paradise Lost*, he cannot bring himself to love the God who would use such power to force submission to His will.

As the baby is buried, Andrew, one of the deacons, pronounces the traditional words that state the orthodox Christian position: "Don' cry, Killdee. De Lawd hab gi' em. De Lawd hab tek em away. Blessed be de name ob de Lawd." Here Andrew represents the conservative forces in the black community that cherish the white man's ancient words and traditions; such blacks do not always understand them, but in their faith they are submissive and unquestioning. Later Maum Hannah, who is helping Rose with the birth of her new child, echoes Andrew when she says, "Some duh comin' an' some duh gwinen. Him up duh tek an' sin. Be tanksful son. Be tanksful."

So life goes on, a new child is born, and the Christians accept the loss of the one who has died. Even Rose is humble; but Killdee, who is now more unregenerate than ever, stares dumbly at Baby Rose's doll and at her cigar-box wagon which lie on the floor. In the conflict with his own conscience, he has not surrendered or mitigated his position.

"Missie" is less of a short story than a connecting bridge between stories. Without "Green Thursday," which serves as partial exposition for this narrative, the reader would not understand sufficiently the feelings of Killdee and Rose toward the "foster daughter" who enters their household. And, without the stories which follow, the conflicts only hinted at in these scenes would seem gratuitous and unresolved.

The sketch "Missie" opens when, shortly after the birth of the baby, a little girl shows up at Killdee's cabin with a bucket of pine chips for Rose. The child, whose name is Missie, is polite and seems willing to work for nothing more than a crust of bread. After questioning her, Rose learns that she is apparently fatherless and comes from an itinerant family who lives nearby in a broken-down shack. Later, when Killdee hears about the girl, he insists that she live with them so that Rose will have someone to help her with the baby. Missie returns with her only possession, her dog Son; and immediately she and Killdee, who is still grieving for his dead daughter, seem to establish a rapport that is vaguely disturbing to Rose. While the animosity between the woman and child is only incipient, the possibility for future rivalry is established. The sketch ends with Missie's awakening after a good night's sleep filled with pleasant dreams of Killdee.

In this episode Mrs. Peterkin displays her novelistic impulses. The scene functions beautifully as an introduction to one of the major characters in a longer work and as the foreshadowing of a significant future conflict. Nothing is overstated. While Rose is reserved toward the girl and instinctively feels a change coming over the household, she is by no means openly hostile. Killdee's pleasure at Missie's arrival can be taken at face value as satisfaction in knowing that Rose will have help; though understood in the light of the previous story, his attitude suggests a smoldering grief and perhaps some alienation from Rose as a result of their bitter words following the baby's death. Missie, who has no last name and who is accustomed to deprivation, finds both security and the father she never had. Yet the potential for trouble is there, ready for development in later scenes.

The virtues of the sketch as an opening scene in a novel are its vices as a short story. Since the essential conflict between the two women is never sufficiently established, there can be no clear-cut statement of a theme that would order the details into a coherent unity. No one in the story is aware of the true significance of the action, and no one comes to any important understanding of himself as a result of the new arrangements. Rose is vaguely aware that something is wrong, but her attitude toward Missie at the end of the scene is not even ambivalent since she cheerfully makes a pallet for the child near the marital bed. When she urges Killdee to leave the child and come to sleep, there is no hint that the tone of her voice is either sarcastic or apprehensive. Missie feels some misgivings about Rose and homesickness for her mother and sister, but the thought of Killdee banishes all regret from her mind. And Killdee simply sees in Missie a companion for Rose and balm for his own grief.

V *Missie and the Church*

In "Meeting," the conflict between the sinners and the saved is reintroduced—this time as it occurs within Missie, who must choose between the world of Killdee and that of Rose. She makes her choice after she attends a prayer meeting and watches the conduct of preacher and congregation with a growing horror that culminates in complete rejection. In the end, having learned about God from Rose and the shouting, weeping church members, she concludes with Killdee that God is cruel and forbidding, something to fear rather than to love.

Here Mrs. Peterkin is able to serve all her aims at once without a conflict of interests. As a sociologist who wants to portray the important qualities of the Gullah, she is able to depict his religion in a fictional scene that is both typical and at the same time unique. The scene is typical because it characterizes the essential ingredients of the Gullah faith—its emotional fervor, its simplicity, its rhetorical excesses; and it is unique because everything is seen from the viewpoint of a wide-eyed and terror-stricken child. In this story, there is none of the preoccupation with quaintness that is found in the works of those writers who attempt to deal with the Southern black community as if they had visited it while on a world tour for the National Geographic Society. Of course, Mrs. Peterkin sometimes indulges in such picturesque cataloguing herself, particularly in portions of

Black April; but in this story all the details have a fictional as well as a sociological purpose.

"Mount Pleasant," like "Missie," is a flimsy bridge between two peaks of action. As a self-contained work of fiction, it lacks several important ingredients. For one thing, there are too many diverse elements to be reconciled thematically within a scant fourteen pages. The central action of the story concerns Missie's first exposure to a primitive baptism and the impact of this experience on her understanding of God and the church. At least one secondary theme is introduced, however—the conflict between the old ways and the new as they are represented, respectively, by Maum Hannah and Rose. While such a conflict is potentially relevant to the central theme of the story, Mrs. Peterkin has not sufficiently developed this potential, particularly in the impressionable mind of the child.

After seeing in the baptismal rite both the possibility of salvation and the winning of Rose's approval, Missie resolves to seek forgiveness and to wait for a sign. Her final thoughts, however, are of Killdee's goodness and of God's arbitrariness which damns the good and rewards the cruel. So the conflict remains to be resolved in "Finding Peace"—the story in which Missie finally unscrambles her confused thoughts and makes an ultimate commitment.

Despite weaknesses as a self-contained short story, "Mount Pleasant" contains some of the finest examples of Mrs. Peterkin's early scenic technique. At this stage of development, the technical management is flawed, as evidenced by the inclusion of irrelevant detail, but one can see in "Mount Pleasant" at least the possibility of the fully developed scenes that give body to *Scarlet Sister Mary.*

"Finding Peace" is the third and final story dealing with Missie's struggle to choose between Rose's way and Killdee's way—the life of the "saint" and the life of the sinner. The child has come to Maum Hannah after she has gone through the traditional period of "seeking," during which she has wandered alone and prayed for a sign of salvation—for a dream or for some unusual occurrence that might be explained in terms of supernatural grace. She is in a rapturous mood as she contemplates the sky and sees in the clouds heaven, God, and the angels; but she has not been concerned with God exclusively during her seeking. Her dress is stained with blackberries and so are her fingers and lips. Her tin pail is full of the fruit, and she intends to sell her harvest at the store and take the money to Rose. She also carries a hat with red trimmings; and red, Maum Hannah later tells her, is not the color to bring peace but to bring trouble. Thus she is still a child of this world, both practical and sensual (natural, as is Killdee).

At first, Maum Hannah is touched to hear that Missie has received a sign and asks her to describe her dream. As the child is speaking, however, the old woman notices the first signs of womanhood and realizes the paradox of Missie's age. At twelve, a young girl is baptized into the church and finds "peace"; but, since she also begins to develop into a woman, her womanhood brings not peace but pain, hardship, and sorrow. Once again religion and nature are in conflict: what religion promises, in its doctrines and ceremonies, natural law implacably forbids. Maum Hannah accepts the paradox, but she feels incapable of making Missie understand.

Missie relates her dream, which seems to Maum Hannah less than extraordinary. The child tells of passing a house where a black woman stood in the door and invited her in to rest. Having refused the woman, she came upon a white house and met a man. When Missie's story trails off into vague details, Maum Hannah becomes suspicious; but the child is evasive because she does not want to admit to the old woman that the man who spoke to her was not God but Killdee. She realizes, of course, that Killdee is a sinner and that sinners could hardly appear in a dream acceptable to the deacons so she leaves Maum Hannah after a few minutes of polite conversation about other matters.

At last Missie's mind is made up. She has found the ceremonies and doctrines of the church too confusing; and, after hearing Maum Hannah, she decides to throw in her lot with the sinners. "After all," she muses, "what difference did it make if she found peace or not? Killdee was a sinner. She'd just stay a sinner with him. Sinners seemed better than Christians, anyway, all except Maum Hannah. And Maum Hannah wasn't a very strict Christian." Missie has found "peace," not by accepting the beliefs and practices of the church but by rejecting them. Once she has decided to abandon her search for salvation through baptism, she is able to love Killdee without reservation and to accept the comfort that his love affords her.

This love is the meaning of her dream after all; for whatever goodness she knows exists in Killdee, and whatever evil she knows exists in Rose, the dark woman at the door, the spokesman for "God." On the surface, Mrs. Peterkin seems to be saying that Rose's God is the crude, anthropomorphic God of the Old Testament, and that the paradox Christ speaks in Matthew xix, 30—"But many that are first shall be last; and the last shall be first"—is true of Killdee. In his kindness toward Missie, Killdee exemplifies the proper Christian spirit ("Inasmuch as ye have done it unto one of the least of these my brethren, ye have done it unto me.") After all Missie's faith is the faith of innocence; and, when she finally casts her lot with Killdee, she suggests that of such faith is the kingdom of heaven.

The theme of these three stories, however, is not quite that simple because Mrs. Peterkin muddies the theological waters with one final scene. Killdee tells Rose to let Missie give up her seeking and return to a normal childhood: "It don't seem natchel fo' Missie to be gwine roun' wid 'e face so long. A-prayin'. Le' em res' off from prayin' an' seekin'." Here Killdee states his own viewpoint, emphasizing the unnatural character of the religious experience. Rose, who sees that she is defeated, agrees to let the child go her own way; and Missie is delighted. She begins to dance around the floor—a violation of church rules—and suddenly feels a sharp stinging in her foot. She has picked up a splinter. Rose immediately insists that God is punishing her for dancing; but Killdee, taking the more pragmatic view, simply gets a penknife and gently removes the tiny sliver.

As in "Green Thursday," the possibility of divine punishment cannot be dismissed; but it seems less likely as an explanation in this story than in the earlier one. The fact remains, however, that to dance—i.e., to live the natural, uninhibited life—is to incur risks, whether supernatural or otherwise; for dancing feet pick up splinters more readily than careful, plodding ones. Perhaps Maum Hannah's vision of Missie's womanhood, coupled with her remarks about the scarlet trimmings, should be juxtaposed with the child's expression of pain as she drops to the floor to examine her foot. Perhaps, on the other hand, Killdee also has the answer to pain— to attack it at its physical source rather than to speculate about its supernatural origins. As in "Green Thursday" and in the other works concerned with theological questions, Mrs. Peterkin does not hand out *ex cathedra* theological answers; therefore, the question of what causes pain in the world remains a moot one.

VI *Life's Hard Lessons*

"The Red Rooster" is perhaps the most unforgettable story in the entire collection, but its principal distinction lies in the naked horror of the climactic scene which is one of the goriest in modern

Southern fiction, a body of literature hardly noted for its squeamishness. Except for that scene, however, the story is strikingly similar to "Green Thursday" because the chief conflict is between the two "world views." However, Killdee and Rose seem less far apart in this story than in "Green Thursday"; and, in the opening scene, they are perhaps significantly so.

In this first scene, Killdee has returned from the evening church meeting and is lying in bed; but he is kept from sleep by the crowing of the red rooster and by the heavy scent of chinaberry blossoms from the tree near his cabin door. He thinks about his foolish attempt to please Rose, who is still suffering the effects of her third childbirth; and he concludes, as always, that the church is no solution for the problems that nature consistently and relentlessly poses: "Being a member could not make old Mike, the mule, younger; or Mike's teeth sound, so he could chew corn and get fat. Mike was too old and slow to keep up with the grass, especially when dog days came and it rained every day God sent. Being a member could not stop that."[6]

When he looks out the window, he sees the new moon through the branches of the chinaberry tree, a sure sign that bad luck will follow. For a few moments, he is disturbed; but he finally concludes that he and Rose have already experienced the worst and dismisses the omen from his mind. As Rose lies in bed, Rose also sees the new moon—floating *above* the chinaberry tree, a sure sign of good luck. She prays to God for her children, first for the baby girl, then for the boy. She also prays for Killdee's conversion, but her prayers are not those of an unquestioning believer. Lying in the darkness, she wonders for a moment if God hears her at all; and then she feels a fear of the darkness and of something more vague and indefinable. Instinctively, she moves closer to Killdee and finally falls asleep under the comforting weight of his heavy arm.

These two interior monologues not only establish the conflict for "Red Rooster" but also suggest a mitigation of both Killdee's viewpoint and Rose's. In view of former tragedies, he does not summarily dismiss superstition on logical grounds; on the other hand, she is not so certain as she once seemed to be that God really exists, much less that He has time for the affairs of lonely, frightened women. Her seeking of Killdee in the darkness, then, exemplifies concretely her human need for him and her proximity (for the moment) to his pragmatic skepticism.

The intermittent crowing of the restless rooster and the stifling scent of the chinaberry blossoms, a reminder of Killdee's first unlucky look at the moon, foreshadow the events which are to follow. The only question is: Whose luck will prevail? And the answer is soon forthcoming. The next day the rooster wakes the baby by crowing at the doorway, and Rose shoos him away in anger, forgetting that he has not been fed. Later he returns, his entrance amply prepared for, and stands before the cradle. In a dramatic stroke, Mrs. Peterkin switches her point of view to that of the rooster, and through his hungry eyes we see what follows:

He was hungry. He had not had a single grain that morning. Not a crumb. Rose and Missie and Killdee had all forgotten to feed him.

The hens were scratching for worms, but it was very hot. They had to hold their wings out away from their bodies while they scratched. A tiresome thing.

Maybe these two, bright shiny eyes would be good to eat. He would have to be quick to get them. They didn't keep still like blackberries. No, but maybe they tasted better.

His yellow beak was sharp and his long neck was strong, and he gave a swift peck. [7]

Outside Rose hears screams and rushes in to find red tears pouring out of a gaping socket where once there had been a brown eye. She picks up the child and stumbles out into the fields where Killdee is plowing up the weeds. There they view the grim work of the rooster; and, as in "Green Thursday," both speculate about the implications of the event. Rose, after defending her own lack of attention to the child, turns on Killdee and berates him for his lack of piety. He in turn remembers the moon behind the chinaberry tree and ascribes the tragedy to bad luck. Always the pragmatist, however, he resolves not only to kill the rooster and to eliminate the final cause but also to chop down the tree and eliminate the first cause as well. He will, in effect, make his own luck.

While "The Red Rooster" is extremely effective as a self-sufficient short story, and while the attitudes of Rose and Killdee are modified to signify at least some small movement in the thematic progress of the continuing narrative, the striking similarities between the structure of "Green Thursday" and this story mitigate to a great extent the effectiveness of the latter and make its thematic development seem all but superfluous. Considered separately, they are two of

Mrs. Peterkin's finest stories. But as sections which form "the thread of a novel," each detracts from the freshness and vitality of the other.

The next story, "Teaching Jim," opens with Killdee's thoughts about Baby Rose (the dead child) as he watches the flame-red glow of the sunset. He remembers the circumstances of her death and his own complicity in it. In this interior monologue, Killdee's new humility is most clearly defined. He vows to himself that he will work hard to provide for his baby son and that he will be extremely careful for the child's sake. And "never again would he stir the earth on Green Thursday. Never." He also reflects, somewhat bitterly, that the boy regards his father as "the greatest thing, the greatest man . . . great as God." To this adulation Killdee can only reply that "Jim didn't know any better."

However humble he may be, Killdee has not lost his sense of the practical. He has noticed that Jim no longer stands near the cabin door because the child has discovered that falling down the steps is a painful experience. Killdee is also aware of Jim's love of the fire, and he decides that the only way to prevent a recurrence of the earlier tragedy is to show Jim how the flame can burn. Despite Rose's weak protest, he takes a glowing coal from the hearth and lays it on the child's fingers. Jim screams, Rose and Missie cry, and Killdee holds the boy in his lap and speculates about the meaning of what he has done. Later, when the child is asleep, he stands outside and wonders if his dead daughter is somewhere in the starry heavens with God.

In this wondering, Killdee seems to have none of the bitterness and antagonism that he feels at the end of "Green Thursday." When he asks the same question in the earlier story, he immediately answers himself with a firm "no." The child is not in heaven; she is lying inside the house on the bed; in effect, there is no immortal soul—only the mortal body. In "Teaching Jim," however, God is at least a possibility to Killdee, a fact he acknowledges to Rose in talking about the death of the baby. His ability to anticipate and to prevent a recurrence of tragedy complements rather than undercuts his new humility, and he seems to find hope in the idea that God helps those who help themselves.

"Teaching Jim" is the most fully developed of all the stories in this collection. In it, naked action is subordinated to scenic rendition; and Mrs. Peterkin builds slowly toward the climactic scene with a series of vivid images which thoroughly define the fire, both as a blessing to be desired and as a danger to be feared. The apparent simplicity of the incident coupled with its thematic scope is ample evidence of Mrs. Peterkin's craftsmanship which, even at this early stage in her development, was singularly impressive despite her brief and informal apprenticeship.

In "Catfish," Killdee's cautious faith in his ability to come to terms with the world is destroyed—and with it his awakening impulse to trust in God. From a man at the country store, he hears that fish make the best natural fertilizer; and he decides to catch enough catfish to bury one under each of his cornstalks to insure a rich yield. The "new" method he discovers is, of course, the oldest in the history of mankind; and its very antiquity gives the story a timeless quality which underlines its universal significance. Maum Hannah, who notes Killdee's frequent trips into the swamp, suspects him of running a still; as a result, she expresses some reservations about the scheme when she hears about it: "I dunno. A buckra might could do 'em. But a nigger—somehow, a nigger don' hab luck when 'e try fo' outdo hisse'f."

Sympathetic, however, Maum Hannah leaves after wishing the scheme well; and the point of view shifts from Killdee to the old woman. That night she awakens to the sound of fighting dogs and a man's whooping voice. Hurrying out to investigate, she finds the cornfield alive with the snarling animals which are digging up the catfish while Killdee, cursing and screaming, runs helplessly among them. Maum Hannah's earlier fears have been confirmed, and she worries about the effects of the defeat on Killdee. "Well," she reasons, "life is like that. She had learned it. Women learn it early. Yes. Men take trouble harder. Harder." When she meets him the next day, she tries to explain that trouble is man's lot; but it is difficult for her to find the words, for she knows that he is young and stubborn. Finally she tells him, "We ain' got no help anywhe' but Up-Yonder, son. We haffer trus' een Him. Haffer!"

Killdee, however, will not accept her philosophy of unquestioning faith. Once again he feels the injustice of natural events and cannot find in his seemingly arbitrary defeat the cause for anything but bitter resentment and outright rejection of all Christian doctrine. He laughs harshly at the old woman and speaks with scorn: "Rose all de time talk de same fool way. Trus' who?"

At this point, the thematic structure of the continuing narrative begins to sag badly. For one thing, the incident—frustrating but not nearly so heart-rending as some of Killdee's earlier experiences—is anticlimactic. To be sure, the pathos of his shattered hopes for an abundant crop is genuine enough, and his backsliding in the light of a long series of tragedies is credible; but no reader can be satisfied to watch indefinitely the same battle being fought and lost, fought and lost again. Eventually pathos gives way to bathos, and the excitement of the conflict is replaced by boredom and annoyance. Only because Mrs. Peterkin's situations are vividly and faithfully portrayed does she escape rejection for these reasons. The truth of the matter is that the potentialities of her theme have been very nearly exhausted insofar as this situation and these characters are concerned.

In "Son," Mrs. Peterkin leaves Killdee's war with God and returns to the related theme of the life-struggle. The story opens when Son, the dog, wakes Killdee with his scratching. Killdee thinks about the dog in terms that suggest he has taken more of Maum Hannah's words to heart: "Fleas had to be. Dogs always had them. Son ought to know that and keep quiet. . . . Son ought to rule himself. To hold steady."[8] Killdee tells Son not to fight the fleas because scratching will tear the dog's hide and bring on the mange which will make him "ugly and mean." In effect, he is telling the dog not to struggle against life's minor adversities or he will expose himself to greater trouble. Killdee, perhaps without realizing it, has begun to adopt the philosophy of acceptance advocated by Maum Hannah and one which Mrs. Peterkin herself seems to consider an essential part of the blacks' code.

The dog, a pure creature of nature (and therefore a perfect counterpart of Killdee as he views himself), leaves the house to follow the scent of a female in heat; and Killdee reflects on the sex instinct and its consequences in dog and man. Son, he tells himself, will have to go far in the cold and dark to find a mate and will probably have to fight other dogs when he gets there. Soon enough he will leave the female and never know his own offspring. Immediately Killdee recognizes the parallel between man and beast; and he thinks of Mary West who has always said, "My chillen daddy ain' nobody een paticular." When Son returns, battered and bloody, Killdee sees the injustice of punishing a creature for pursuing fulfillment of its natural desires. "Who was to blame?" he asks himself. "What? Why couldn't things be fair to dogs?—and to men—and women?"

Then, in a passage that seems abrupt and underdeveloped, Killdee thinks of Missie; and one realizes for the first time that his feelings towards the girl are more than paternal:

A face came before Killdee's eyes—black—eager—young—with a bluish bloom on the cheeks—a pointed chin where a dimple came and went—dark red lips where white teeth gleamed with laughter—lips that quivered in such a pitiful way when things went wrong—little Missie—good little Missie.

She was so little—so tender—so trustful. Could he ruin her because she was what he loved best?

Love was a disease. It was wilting all the joy in her—in himself. It was a poison that would burn and shrivel—that would change her clean freshness to shame.[9]

The implications of this passage are clear—Killdee is in love with Missie. What has seemed an affection of a father for a daughter has turned into a love colored by sexual desire. In recognizing the beast in himself, he acknowledges the true nature of his feelings; for, like Son, he is an animal driven by natural desires that are all but uncontrollable. And yet, in man, he reflects, they are controllable. Like the dog, who licks his wounds and heals himself, man too should be able to cure his hurts. Because, as he finally realizes, "hurt," or trouble, is the immitigable law of nature; and this law is indigenous not only to man and beast but to the most elemental things of earth: "Me and Son ain' de onlies' one hab trouble. Mud puddle hab 'em too. 'E can' be still. 'E haffer stan' pain. De wind trouble em. De sun-hot'll dry em up. Po' mud puddle! Do Jedus!"

As if to prove this philosophical generalization, Son, who is hungry for meat, ventures into the swamp and loses a leg in one of Killdee's traps that have been set out for the same reasons that have brought Son into such perilous country. Killdee's bitterness emerges again as he reasons that Son was not merely scratching fleas or seeking a mate; he was trying to survive. This incident, then, represents the nature of the life-struggle: in the very act of self-preservation (as well as in that of procreation), a creature encounters mortal danger; and Killdee reflects that the inevitable end of such a struggle is death, both for man and beast.

In addition to the redundancy of thematic statement, this story suffers from a structural weakness that is unjustifiable, even if one takes the novelistic framework into account. The introduction of sexuality into Killdee's feelings toward Missie is inadequately prepared for; and, consequently, it fails to function as an integral part of the story *qua* story or as a valid development in the continuing action. From a realistic standpoint, of course, such a development is quite credible, perhaps even inevitable, because of the circumstances of Rose and Killdee's marriage.

VII *Killdee Has His Way*

In "A Sunday," Killdee finds out much to his surprise that Rose has become involved with the "stylish" young preacher, Mr. Felder, whom she has invited home for Sunday dinner. The purveyor of this gossip, promiscuous Mary West, obviously has her own motives for wishing to alienate Killdee from Rose; but the rumors are circulating among all the negroes in the quarter; and Killdee, who has noticed a change in Rose, recognizes that some truth exists in what is being said. Consequently, he goes to Daddy Cudjoe, the old "conjure man," for advice; but all Daddy can tell him is to rely on his own judgment and to remember that fear is a man's greatest enemy. Killdee admits that he is afraid of the laughter of others; and, when he resolves to put his fears behind him, Daddy Cudjoe gives him one more piece of advice: "Dese preacher, dese member, all dese Christian, dey is 'f'aid too! You 'member dat! You mus'n' be 'f'aid dem! Not no mo'."[10]

On his way home, Killdee learns that the deacons are planning to discuss the matter publicly at the next Sunday meeting and to dismiss Rose from the congregation as a sinner. When he arrives home, Rose is malingering and is lying in bed with a collard leaf tied on her supposedly pain-wracked head. The scene which follows is essentially humorous, despite its serious import both to Rose and to Killdee. He does not confront her openly with the stories he has heard; instead, he toys with her in feigned innocence:

"I t'ink so much ch'ch ain' good fo' you." Rose moved and sniffled again, but said nothing. "Whe' Revern' Felder? 'E ain' come home wid you? At you fix so much fine eatin' fo' eb e ain' come?" " 'E ain' come to Mount Pleasant to-day. 'E sen' a answer 'e mighty sick," Rose answered humbly. "Howcome you hab de haid-ache? You mus be eat too much."[11]

Rose pretends illness all week; and, on the following Sunday, she breaks all precedent by staying in bed. Killdee, however, dresses in his best clothes, and he departs an hour before church time. He goes straight to Mount Pleasant; and, after waiting for the prayers to end, he strides to the pulpit, turns on the congregation, and tells them in a quiet, pleasant voice that he knows what the meeting is about and that he has only one thing to say: "De fus' nigger eber call my wife name een dis chu'ch is got to deal wid me! Me! Killdee Pinesett! Da's all."

As he speaks to them he realizes the truth of what Daddy Cudjoe has told him: the "Christians" are all afraid. Their self-righteousness and their false piety wither before his firm gaze, for he has put the matter on a personal basis, and there can be no safety in numbers. The results of the confrontation are as Killdee has planned; and, though the congregation sends word to Reverend Felder that he is never to come to Mount Pleasant again, Rose remains a member in good standing because, in order to turn her out, someone would have to call her by name. News soon comes that Reverend Felder is dead, a victim of lockjaw that developed as a result of a mysterious wound in the leg. Shaken by this information, no one will dare speculate about how the reverend came to be wounded or at whose hands.

"A Sunday," as a self-contained work of fiction, is something more than an anecdote; but it does not achieve complete success as a short story. For one thing, the reader never knows how Rose feels about Killdee's actions, nor is there any indication of what the future relationship between the two will be. Indeed, the reader must question to what extent Killdee has been affected by Rose's dalliance. His pride is stung, of course; but, after his talk with Daddy Cudjoe, he seems to have put aside such considerations; and, when he presents himself before the congregation, he does so as a man who has mastered all doubts and fears. The subsequent death of Reverend Felder, however, would suggest otherwise, though the author does not explore the subtlety of Killdee's feelings toward the interloper, nor indeed does she confirm absolutely that Killdee is responsible for the fatal wound. Thus once again the narrative lacks sufficient character delineation and a satisfactory resolution.

As far as the continuing action is concerned, however, "A Sunday" is a welcome relief from the sections that immediately precede it. For one thing, the variety of subject matter is refreshing. The action is concerned with the relationship between the main characters and the community rather than with a character's struggle with nature for survival or with the conflict over belief in a supernatural God. While these primary concerns of the earlier stories are vital and basic, the role of the community in such concerns is also extremely important; its exploration gives the series of natural

tragedies extra dimension since Killdee must not only struggle with
the forces of impersonal nature but also must come to terms with the
demands of human society. That Mrs. Peterkin can present these
demands so humorously and so in contrast with the grimness of her
primary mode suggests that she had the instincts of a good novelist
even in the early stages of her development.

"Plum Blossoms," the final episode in the book, is Mrs. Peterkin's
attempt to resolve all of the various conflicts introduced earlier
without compromising the dignity of her central characters more
than is absolutely necessary. The plum blossoms, because of their
early appearance, their white purity, and their delicate fragrance
are clearly identified with Missie. Killdee, who first encounters the
blossoms on his way home from plowing, finds that his mournful
reflection about the pain and monotony of life are suddenly replaced
with a strange exhilaration. At home, Missie has decorated the
house with the white blossoms which have already begun to shed on
the floor. Rose, who is annoyed because Missie has put on a clean
white dress for Killdee, orders the girl to sweep the floor and then
angrily berates her for laziness and a lack of proper respect.

The conflict between the two females lies barely beneath the
surface of their dialogue, and it almost breaks into the open when
Rose accuses Missie of having no regard for Killdee. At this moment, the girl abandons her submissiveness and begins to defend
herself, finally shouting in her frustration, "Ef you tell Killdee dat,
you is a lie." At this instant Killdee comes in; and Rose, who begins
to present her side of the quarrel, convinces him that Missie has, to
some extent, been disrespectful. Rose demands punishment, and he
is forced to make a decision which is, in effect, a choice between the
two women. For a moment he wavers; he's angry with the girl for
her disobedience and seeming lack of gratitude, but he's reluctant to
strike her with the thick leather trace which she herself has polished
for him only that day as evidence of her love. After the strap falls to
the floor and he releases Missie, he rushes outside with Rose's
taunts ringing in his ears and is smothered with the scent of plum
blossoms.

He feels trapped—by his love for Missie, by life itself. But he is
not sure that he wants to escape. In the distance he hears the words
of an old hymn which the congregation sings at the evening meeting, "I'm-so-glad/My trouble—won' las'-always."[12] These words express old Christian optimism with its promise of an ultimate end to

sorrow; but to Killdee, who feels himself to be an alien in an uncaring universe, the words suggest a different meaning: "Joy can' las' always needer. You sing about trouble. I'm gwine take one joy whilst I kin."[13] His meaning seems to be clear. He will take Missie, whatever the consequences; for, as a more sophisticated poet has put it, "Luck's a chance but trouble's sure."[14] Moreover, the Christian ethic, with its emphasis on self-denial, is predicated on the existence of a God in whom Killdee, on the basis of his own bitter experience, cannot believe.

Thus, in the final analysis Killdee is unchanged; he is as skeptical in the last episode as in the first. There are moments during the course of the continuing narrative when he seems to move closer to Rose's first, childish, unquestioning faith; but such impulses, only short-lived, are based on a temporary triumph that is soon erased by the inevitable defeats which follow. As he stands on the porch and breathes the fragrance of the plum blossoms, Killdee's hopes are simple and basic—some modicum of beauty and love to enable him to endure the inevitable sorrows that are his lot.

VIII   *In Summary*

Green Thursday, despite its weaknesses, must be regarded as an extraordinary performance for a writer as untrained and inexperienced as Mrs. Peterkin. Most first novels are imitative and therefore lacking in those distinctive qualities of style and characterization that are characteristic of genuinely significant fiction. But Mrs. Peterkin's plantation world is all her own, and out of the Gullah dialect and her close observation of black speech she devises both dialogue and a narrative prose that suggest without slavishly imitating the language and thoughts of her characters. Killdee, Rose, and Missie have no counterparts in other plantation fiction, because the blacks of the South Carolina low country have their own customs, superstitions, and philosophy and because Mrs. Peterkin patterned them after real people whom she had known intimately for many years.

Indeed, *Green Thursday* reveals a simple power and grace that derives from its apparent lack of any literary antecedent. Working alone with no more than an occasional word of advice from the outside, she was able to suit the work to the subject with an unselfconsciousness that was a strength as well as a weakness; and while her linked narratives are spare and straightforward, they have some-

thing of the evocative power of the lyric poetry written during this
same period.

While the book was by no means a best seller, the critical response, as noted in Chapter One, was generally enthusiastic, and
Mrs. Peterkin was treated as a writer addressing herself to serious
sociological and fictional problems rather than as a talented amateur
or local colorist. And the critics were right. *Green Thursday* is a
genuine work of art; and its author, pleased that it was so received,
began to think of trying her talents on a more ambitious project.

CHAPTER 3

Oedipus in the Low Country

B*lack April*[1] is one of those American novels—like Herman Melville's *Moby Dick*, Scott Fitzgerald's *The Great Gatsby*, and Robert Penn Warren's *All the King's Men*—that chronicles the downfall of a hero as it is viewed through the eyes of a character who is only peripherally involved in the action. In Mrs. Peterkin's narrative, the "hero" is the black plantation foreman April who rules his domain like a medieval prince: he takes whichever women he wants; he fights all would-be usurpers (including his son and chief rival, Sherry); and, finally, in his arrogance, he incurs the curse of an old conjure woman whose spell seems to bring his illness and death. The character who watches this spectacle is Breeze, the young boy; and through him we understand the true nature of April's fall— which is essentially tragic.

I *Tragedy*

Tragedy, however defined, has traditionally been the highest goal of serious writers; and it is small wonder that Julia Peterkin, who at this stage of her career thought she would write only one novel, should try to make the most of her own experience on Lang Syne and create something of a tragedy in *Black April*. Mrs. Peterkin, always modest in her literary pretensions, did not, of course, announce her purpose either in private correspondence or in overt literary allusions that would invite comparison with the great Classical tragedies. But the character of her hero, the nature of his conflict, and the course of the action in which he is involved—all these elements bear striking witness to the seriousness of her intent; and her handling of the hero's downfall is so similar in technique to the method of others' tragedies that it is difficult not to believe she knew precisely what she was doing.

As evidence that she did, it is interesting to compare, for example, Professor Northrop Frye's definition of the high mimetic hero of Classical epic and tragedy with Mrs. Peterkin's central character: "If superior in degree to other men but not to his natural environment, the hero is a leader. He has authority, passions, and powers of expression far greater than ours, but what he does is subject both to social criticism and to the order of nature. This is the hero of the *high mimetic* mode, of most epic and tragedy, and is primarily the kind of hero that Aristotle had in mind."[2]

Such a character is also the kind of hero that Mrs. Peterkin had in mind when she wrote *Black April*. The novel's protagonist, April, is certainly superior to all others on the fictional plantation Blue Brook. He is six feet four, a match for any man half his age when it comes to physical combat; he has a superior knowledge about all the lore that is relevant to the primitive plantation society in which he lives; and he possesses a sense of his own power and masculinity that makes him irresistible to the women of the community. For these reasons, he is the foreman—the leader of his people—and the law itself for an entire self-contained society. His pride and arrogance, however, which are part of his superiority, also subject him to criticism; and he alienates one after another of his friends and subordinates—indeed, he incurs their curses. And he is also subject to the laws of nature—a nature that, according to the community in which he lives, is the agent of mysterious cosmic moral forces that eventually destroy all those who defy them.

Such a man then, is April; but what makes a hero tragic, as opposed to comic or epic? Having classified fictional heroes, Professor Frye is able to apply those classifications to what he calls "the tragic mode" and to supply five neatly packaged answers to such a question. The answer of relevance to *Black April* is the one which deals with "high mimetic" tragedy:

> Tragedy in the central or high mimetic sense, the fiction of the fall of a leader (he has to fall because that is the only way in which a leader can be isolated from his society), mingles the heroic with the ironic. In elegiac romance the hero's mortality is primarily a natural fact, the sign of his humanity; in high mimetic tragedy it is also a social and moral fact. The tragic hero has to be of a properly heroic size, but his fall is involved both with a sense of his relation to society, and with a sense of the supremacy of natural law, both of which are ironic in reference. Tragedy belongs chiefly to the two indigenous developments of tragic drama in fifth-century

Athens and seventeenth-century Europe from Shakespeare to Racine. Both belong to a period of social history in which an aristocracy is fast losing its effective power but still retains a good deal of ideological prestige.[3]

In this statement, one can see the nature of the "fall" which Aristotle called "nemesis." It is isolation from society, as Professor Frye defines it, and also disharmony with nature and with those moral forces that inform nature. From this isolation and disharmony grow the circumstances which lead to the hero's destruction—to his fall from a position of preeminence. In *Black April,* the foreman defies community opinion and is contemptuous of religious strictures. The result is his public humiliation, his loss of his position of leadership, and, eventually, his death.

In order to render this tragic action, Mrs. Peterkin's problem was twofold: first, to establish a moral order against which her hero, April, can be broken; and, second, to create the world of an isolated South Carolina plantation in colors vivid and compelling enough for the reader to accept it as reality. In order to solve this problem, the author had to resort to certain technical devices. At times, she achieved only partial success; but that she ultimately succeeded in creating a believable fictional world and an action that in its essence approximates tragedy is a tribute to her intelligence and to her instinctive literary genius.

The reader sees the working out of Mrs. Peterkin's dilemma in the two part structure of the novel. The first two-thirds of the book is almost (but not quite) singlemindedly devoted to the definition of the Gullah world. The last one-third is the story of April, his downfall, and its effect on the community and on Breeze, who is both an onlooker and a participant in the action. While she is establishing the framework for her tragic action, Mrs. Peterkin makes little attempt to create the illusion of plot development; therefore, the first part of the novel is relatively static while the second part is characterized by rapid movement.

II *Point of View and The Preparation for Tragedy*

The character of Breeze, April's illegitimate son, provides Mrs. Peterkin with the perfect device to introduce her fictional world. For one thing, Breeze is a little boy whose knowledge of his social milieu is largely self-conscious. Like all children, he spends his first few years assimilating the culture into which he has been born; and he must consciously take note of the do's and don't's that such adults as his cousin Big Sue, Maum Hannah, and April impress upon him. As these older "initiates" reveal the world of Blue Brook to the "uninitiated" Breeze, they also define this world for the reader; and Mrs. Peterkin need not apologize for analytical and discursive passages since they are dramatically justifiable as a part of Breeze's education concerning the ways of plantation life.

Thus, though Mrs. Peterkin begins her story prior to the boy's birth in order to give the reader some essential information about his origins, the reader is soon viewing the world through Breeze's eyes as the boy goes to live with Cousin Big Sue, the cook at the Big House; and, in a series of vignettes involving knowledgeable adults, the various facets of plantation life are explored. Indeed, in the first two-thirds of the novel, the method is that of a grade school primer in which Dick and Jane learn the grammar of home, farm, and nation.

In Chapter V, the schooling begins with a lesson about the plantation and the white people who own it. Big Sue and Uncle Isaac, the aged patriarch and April's predecessor as foreman, explain to Breeze that the White House that stands at the heart of the land belongs to the "buckra," that they are absentee landlords, and that they come to hunt duck and deer only during the cool weather when they are safe from swamp fever. Thus Mrs. Peterkin is able to justify to her readers the absence of a racial confrontation that is the essence of so much fiction about the American Negro and to explain at the same time the existence of the plantation and the presence of the blacks on it.

In Chapter VI, Uncle Bill, one of Big Sue's several nocturnal callers, is introduced to Breeze; and the boy begins to see something of the ritual of courtship which plays an important part in the later action. As Uncle Bill and Big Sue exchange playful banter, they illustrate the easy morality of the Gullahs and their preoccupation even in old age with sexual matters. These three characters are soon joined by Zeda, a creation who is recognizable as the Scarlet Sister Mary of Mrs. Peterkin's next novel; and Breeze begins to hear the gossip that is the spice of plantation social life. Some of the talk concerns April and his jealous wife, Leah; some concerns Big Sue's estranged husband, whose absence is merely convenient; and some concerns Zeda's ten children, no two with the same father. By the end of such conversation, the "informality" of sexual arrangements is defined well enough to provide a framework for the later relationships that develop between April and the various plantation women.

In Chapter VII, the first real meeting between Breeze and April occurs; and the boy sees for the first time the operation of such law as there is in Blue Brook. The scene is a "birth night supper," one of the most important social rites among the Gullahs; and, after considerable drinking and frenzied dancing, two young rivals exchange heated words, and a knife appears. April, as foreman, steps forward; and, in a gesture of fine contempt for the younger men, he orders that they be thrown out of the dance hall. It is immediately apparent to Breeze and to the reader that brute force rules on the plantation.

In a settlement far too remote for the exercise of duly constituted legal authority, the foreman must settle all disputes that threaten either the economic welfare or the domestic tranquility of the community; and only the man physically equipped to perform such a task holds such a position. When his strength fails him or when someone else appears who can demonstrate superior prowess, the foreman is supplanted by the better man; and a new cycle of authority is begun. The role of the white man in these matters seems to be negligible, a simple ratification of the status quo; and later in the narrative, when the young black Sherry replaces April as foreman, the choice is, in effect, made by the blacks themselves. Sherry, they know, has the ability to whip the other men into line and to keep the system in operation. As a result of such incidents, the "political" structure of Blue Brook is primitive and tribal. The chief, as in all primitive tribes, is the man who is best able to lead the group in that activity that sustains its existence; and, since plantation farming requires the cooperative effort of the entire community—men, women, children—the abnegation of responsibility by the white owner forces the blacks of Blue Brook to resort to these ancient and primal methods of choosing a leader.

In Chapter VIII, Breeze begins to see nature as it is viewed through the eyes of his people. Big Sue initiates the lesson with a stroll through the garden during which she tells the boy about all the flowers and shrubbery. The garden, which had once been a close-clipped and formal one, is now undisciplined since the white people no longer live on the premises. The old way of life, beautiful but impractical, has given way to the new; and the severe formality of white attitudes and manners has been supplanted by the more exuberant and natural black ways. In a series of vignettes which

extend into Chapter IX, Big Sue fills Breeze's spinning head with
some of the most fascinating and valuable folklore to be found in
literature about the black. If a trumpet vine waves at you, you must
bow back. Bluejays go to hell every Friday with a stick of wood to
stoke the devil's fires. If you walk along behind someone and step in
his tracks, you will give him a headache or a toothache. To stop such
a pain, the person responsible for the discomfort must break a stick
in two and cross the broken pieces. Carrying oak-galt or buckeyes
will cure rheumatism.

These scenes are obviously intended by Mrs. Peterkin for the
chronicling of Gullah superstitions, but she indulges her delight in
the picturesque to the detriment of balance and proportion in the
structure of her novel. The chronicle is, to some extent, functional
since it defines the view of nature held by the Gullahs—a view that
prepares for Breeze's attitude toward the events of the narrative.
But the pouring of so many bits and pieces of lore into such a small
mold tends to strain the ingenuity of the writer and the patience and
credulity of the reader. As a result, Mrs. Peterkin becomes less the
novelist than the folklorist, and the illusion of fictional reality is
broken in places.

In Chapter X, the superstitions catalogued are those relating to
barnyard animals; and the essence of the Gullah world view is most
clearly revealed in them as the primitivism that it is. Christianity
does not lie at the heart of this view but a belief in magic that
antedates the earliest tribal religion and even such ancient attitudes
as totemism and animism. After Big Sue finishes with him, Breeze
seems to accept without question this primitive view of nature; and
Chapter X ends his education by the women of the community.
They have taught him the history of the plantation; its rules and
customs; their views of sex, of marriage, and of the lore concerning
most of the creatures found in the barnyard. Now they surrender
him to April, Sherry, and Uncle Bill, who introduce him to the
masculine world.

In Chapter XI, Sherry takes the young boy 'possum hunting, and
then April invites him to go on a turkey shoot. In the scene that
follows, which is one of the most significant in the novel, the boy
learns from his father a lesson of courage in the face of danger and
death—a lesson that is the essence of the initiation in all primitive
tribes. In Breeze's case, no ritualistic ceremony occurs such as those
found in many of the Indian tribes and in primitive Africa even

today; but the archetypal meaning of the scene that involves him is quite clear.

As the father and son sit in the blind with shotguns and wait for the wild turkeys to fly in, April smells a rattlesnake nearby. After stalking the creature in tall grass, he sees it, snatches it up in his hand, and stares into its eyes. In a loud voice he speaks to the snake, proclaiming that his blue gums have a potent poison; and then he spits defiantly into the fanged mouth. After doing so, he demands that Breeze, who has blue gums, also spit down the snake's throat. Breeze is frightened and misses the first time, but the second time he is successful; and April praises him as one who has more courage than the older Sherry.

The snake's traditional symbolic significance in this incident is apparent. In confronting the open mouth and poisonous fangs, Breeze is confronting evil (or death) itself; and, in showing his defiance, he is proving his courage and therefore his manhood. It is right and proper that such an initiation—whether formal or informal—should be ministered by the boy's father; and, having proven himself worthy of the company of men, Breeze is allowed to go with Sherry and Uncle Bill on a duck hunt. First, however, April introduces him to the masculine world of guns and weapons by taking him into the Big House and helping him to choose a shotgun. Then, the next morning, the adventure begins, with a warning from Uncle Bill: "Mind, son. Don' put you' hand on Miss Big Sue. When a man is gwine a-huntin', it'll ruin his luck to let a lady touch him. Be careful!" Thus the clear division is made between the work of woman and that of man; and, like some primitive old warrior whose pride is in his manliness, Uncle Bill passes along the admonition to the young boy that the touch of a woman (effeminacy) is a curse when man's work is to be done.

Thus, in this chapter Breeze learns about the life-struggle—learns to kill with a certain proficiency tempered by pity; and, while he is doing so, Uncle Bill and Sherry fill his head with the beliefs and superstitions which comprise the lore of Gullah men; and they thereby complement all that Big Sue has taught him. Once again, Mrs. Peterkin is the amateur folklorist; and, while the conversation is functional for reasons already suggested, she includes too much superstition for the action to absorb. As a result, the reader becomes painfully aware of the author's sociological intent before the scene ends.

At the end of Chapter XIV, in which Breeze goes to a church meeting, the lengthy exposition of the Gullah world is complete; for, by the conclusion of this evening, he has absorbed most of the significant lore of the plantation community—that knowledge which helps him to see society and nature through the eyes of the Blue Brook Gullah. Whatever questions remain in the mind of the central character or the reader—the relationship between primitive superstition and Christianity, for instance—are questions that either need no answers or have none; and the action that takes place in the last one-third of the book has been thoroughly "undergirded" by the information provided in the first two-thirds.

III   Plot: The Tragic Action

While the primary function of the first sections of Black April is to provide a comprehensive description of life on Blue Brook Plantation, Mrs. Peterkin also introduces significant themes and begins to define her central characters and the primary conflict of the novel. Thus, when Breeze learns about "law" on Blue Brook at the birth night supper, the reader also sees April's high-handed humiliation of the young men—action that foreshadows his fight with Sherry. A character such as Big Sue, used as a means of conveying information to the reader about Gullah customs and beliefs, also serves as an example of the women over whom April has sexual dominion. And, while Sherry and Uncle Bill tell Breeze about the ways of the hunter, they also talk about April's "long legs" and about the hatred that Sherry holds for the foreman. In these and other scenes the author begins to spin the first threads of a plot which takes definite shape only after two-thirds of the book is over; but, as has been noted, the dominant business in these earlier sections is that of exposition.

April, of course, is the main character, the "tragic hero"; and the plot is constructed around him—as the title of the book suggests. Breeze is the "telescope" through whom the reader views April; but, if he were not something more than that, there would be little excuse in wasting so much space on his thoughts and actions; what matters is their relationship to April. After all, a good many of the incidents in the book involve the young boy's sensibilities, his initiation into the adult world, and his relationship with characters other than his father. To assume that these incidents have no thematic relevance to the main plot is to assume that the novel is an imperfect fusion of two separate narratives.

Such is not the case, for what Breeze finally learns from all the experiences he undergoes is precisely what April never learned—a sense of humility in the face of the moral order as embodied in the community and in the church. To be sure, Breeze shows much of his father's independence at the end of the narrative, even to the point of momentarily forgetting his religious impulses; but the last chapter, "Seeking," suggests that April's final end makes its impact on Breeze; indeed, April's fate is the climax of all the lessons Breeze has learned from the day of his advent to Blue Brook.

Like Ishmael in *Moby Dick*, Nick Carraway in *The Great Gatsby*, and Jack Burden in *All the King's Men*, Breeze remains after the protagonist is dead as a symbol of the return to moral order—for he renounces the sin that has brought about the hero's downfall. But April is still the character who inspires pity and terror in Breeze as well as in the reader; and Breeze's story has meaning and purpose only because of April's. Despite the ultimate importance of April, however, Breeze does not encounter his father until Chapter VII, when he is at the birth night supper and sees April as the very embodiment of the legends circulated about him. April appears suddenly at the celebration to offer Big Sue a drink of whisky in contempt of church prohibitions; and, when he sees Breeze trying to peer through the window at the dancers, he hoists the little boy up "as if he were no heavier than a feather." When the fight breaks out, April roars a threat and peace is restored. He is the keeper of order, the absolute authority, the "king."

At the end of the evening, Big Sue asks April to walk home with them—obviously an invitation that has implications the boy fails to grasp; but April declines, saying that he does not want to "get in Uncle Bill's way." Two chapters later, however, he appears on a Saturday afternoon to eat fish with Big Sue; and he suggests afterward that the boy find something to occupy him elsewhere. The meaning of these and other such scenes is obvious. By virtue of his strength and power April has his way with Big Sue and with other women on the plantation.

At the end of Chapter IX, the white storekeeper[4] warns Big Sue that she will find trouble if she continues to consort with April; and his warning is the first hint the reader has that trouble is on the way. The scene in which April teaches Breeze to spit in the mouth of the snake is also significant in terms of the tragic line of the plot, for the pride of the foreman manifests itself in the very teeth of evil. His defiance, his assertion of superiority over the snake, is one more link in the chain of events that define his hubris. The pride he feels in his own manhood and his enjoyment of that masculine prowess lead him to imagine that he is superior to the natural and supernatural forces around him. He is soon to learn, in a lesson almost as bitter as that of Oedipus, how wrong he is.

In the next chapter, the explicit nature of that lesson is foreshadowed; but the terms are so oblique that only at the end is the meaning obvious. Sherry and Uncle Bill take Breeze duck hunting; and, while on the lake, the three of them meet April. Everyone exchanges pleasantries, but April and Sherry seem hostile to each other; and for the second time Breeze sees the foreman impugn the younger man's masculinity: "When did you get so pa'ticular, Sherry? You must be kissed you' elbow an' turned to a lady, enty?" After April has left, Uncle Bill asks Sherry why he doesn't like April; and Sherry, after pausing to reflect, says,

> "April's legs is most too long fo' de foreman of a big plantation like Blue Brook."
> "Wha' you mean, son?"
> "Dey kin tote him too far f'om home sometimes."
> "You mean April kin walk too far atter dark?"
> "Yes suh." Uncle Bill sighed.
> "Gawd is de one made 'em long. April ain' had nothin' to do wid dat. Gawd made you' own not so short, Sherry. Don' fo'git dat."[5]

This scene is crucial; brief though it is, it bears a heavy thematic burden since it not only establishes the important conflict between April and Sherry (April is later to marry Sherry's girl, Joy) but also defines April's legs as symbolic of his masculine sexuality. Thus the scene prepares the reader for the denouement in which April's legs are "cursed," become gangrenous, and are amputated.

In Chapter XIV, April courts disaster by displaying a contempt for the beliefs and ceremonies of the church, though his hubris here is mitigated to some extent by the fact that the preacher is little more than a confidence man who is using the faith and ignorance of the congregation to collect money. In a twist that is unexpected (and, for the most part, insignificant), the charlatan turns out to be Breeze's former "stepfather" who left the boy's mother after Old Breeze had died and after he had dug up the grandfather's buried savings. There is, perhaps, a hint of foul play about the old man's death since no one is ever sure how he fell into the river; but the reader is never given the key to unlock the mystery, and the whole business is so extraneous to the main action that no one really cares.

The important fact is that the preacher is using the new Bury League as a device to collect money from the gullible church members and that April challenges the newcomer's authority before the entire congregation in a manner that violates the sanctity of the church. Of course, the preacher has already revealed himself as something less than a "professional" during the course of the service. As he is shouting the ten commandments and as the congregation is responding, Maum Hannah suddenly screams that he is reciting them incorrectly. And, sure enough, in his fervor he is telling the assembly, "Thou shalt kill. Thou shalt commit adultery. Thou shalt steal. Thou shalt bear false witness against thy neighbor." When April hears this slip of the tongue, he breaks into a "cool, sneering smile" and then rises in the middle of the service to leave. All present are shocked at the foreman's lack of manners—in effect, by his failure to observe religious propriety—but the service soon regains its feverish emotional pitch. After the sermon, the offering, and the communion, all repair to the yard for refreshments.

There a ludicrous accident occurs that brings the conflict between preacher and foreman to a head. Leah, April's wife, accidentally drops her "store-bought" teeth into the barrel of lemonade prepared for the occasion; and, after some discussion and attempts to retrieve the dentures, the members of the refreshment committee agree that they will wait until the level of the liquid has been lowered. Having come to this conclusion, they courteously offer the preacher the first drink; and, when he refuses, April suddenly appears and challenges him. April is, of course, assuming an insult where there is none in order to provoke the preacher into a fight, probably because this outsider is a threat to the status quo at Blue Brook. When Uncle Bill warns against butting a "servant of Gawd" and suggests that April will be struck dead, the foreman replies, "I doubt if Gawd would knock me 'bout dat, but I don' b'lieve I want to dirty my skull on such a jackass."

The fracas that follows ends when April bites a hunk of flesh out of the preacher's cheek and spits it out for a hound to gobble up. Everyone is shocked, including Breeze, who, though he knows the background of the preacher, is convinced that the Lord will indeed strike his father dead. April, contemptuous to the last, clears his throat, spits, and walks away, "Cool. Master of himself. Alone."

April's action, though partially justified by the preacher's dubious
background and intentions, undermines April's character in the
eyes of Breeze; and in the next chapter the boy turns against his
father completely. The occasion is an incident in the cottonfield
when the smoldering quarrel between April and Sherry bursts into
violent flame. Sherry defends Breeze from the attack of an older
bully; and, when the foreman comes to investigate, the two
headstrong men begin to argue. April finally grabs Sherry, butts
him in the head, and then orders him off the plantation.

Since Sherry has been defending Breeze and since April's true
motive for banishing Sherry is unknown to the boy (April fears the
younger man, both as a challenger of his absolute authority and as a
competitor for the favors of plantation women), Breeze is suddenly
filled with a deep resentment. Sherry, his nose bleeding and tears
streaming down his cheeks, hurls a curse at April which is a grim
prophecy: "You stinkin' ugly devil . . . . You's got a coward-heart
even if you' head is too tough fo' Hell! I hope Gawd'll rot all two o'
you feets off! I hope E will—"[6]

The other men tell Sherry to hush, to leave quietly; but their own
silence after he has gone suggests their unhappiness and their disapproval of April. And, as Breeze gazes across the fields at Sherry
leaving, the scene becomes dark and ominous to his eyes. Already
powers are at work, and April's moment of supreme reign is ending.
As in *Green Thursday*, Mrs. Peterkin does not commit herself entirely to a supernatural explanation of April's downfall. But, like
Nathaniel Hawthorne—the first great equivocator in American
literature—she also does not insist on a naturalistic interpretation.
The curse has been hurled at April by Sherry; and it is to be repeated by Sherry's mother, Zeda, in a manner much more diabolic
than hysterical. But, before the reader sees the repetition of the
curse and the punishment of April's pride, Mrs. Peterkin injects two
scenes which, though they are digressions, reinforce the main action
thematically in that they are concerned with death—that resolver of
most human problems.

The first scene is an adaptation of "Manners," a brilliant *Reviewer*
sketch in which a frightened girl is forced to look into the face of her
dead mother in order to learn self-control. In *Black April*, it is
Breeze's mother who has died; but the incident, in all its horror,
remains essentially the same as the one in the short story. The face
of death which the boy sees as he stares into his mother's sightless
eyes is the same face that he sees at the end when his father is lying

on his deathbed. And the lesson that Big Sue impresses upon him—too cruelly perhaps—is the lesson of control. One must show "manners," the respect for one's elders and for the power of God that eventually destroys and redeems all men. There is something of the Conradian concept of "code" in Big Sue's attitude, but there is also something there of traditional *pietas*—a curious mixture that seems closer to Faulkner than to contemporary writers, such as Joseph Hergesheimer, for whom Mrs. Peterkin expressed admiration.

The second significant incident concerned with death is one in which the ritual of the hog killing is described. The sacrificial victim is Jeems, who is Big Sue's beloved shoat; and the entire process is described from beginning to end— the preparation, the stroke of the knife, the agonizing squeal, and the careful dissection of the animal's carcass to utilize virtually every part, including hooves and bones. There is, in this scene, a celebration of death that is ancient and meaningful. The heart of the life-struggle is given form and dignity on this occasion when, despite Breeze's pity for the frightened animal, Jeems is slashed to pieces that others might continue to live. Indeed, the meaning of the scene is underlined by the fact that Joy, Big Sue's daughter, has returned pregnant with Sherry's child; and everyone believes that the freshly killed meat will be good for her constant nausea (though the true nature of her condition is unknown to the community). The name "Joy" and the new life that stirs within her suggest the ancient and proper reasons for the sacrifice; and what might be a cold, disgusting business in the slaughter houses of Swift and Armour is—among a people closely in communion with nature and her immutable laws of survival—a bright, festive occasion tempered only by a sense of pity for the victim of their necessity.

After the hog killing is over, the butchered Jeems is hung outside the door and is promptly stolen. When Leah, who has already fought with Big Sue once, indicates her amusement at the theft, the two women fight again; and Breeze notes that Leah falls to the floor with the same look that Jeems had in his eyes. Indeed, Leah is dead; but since the consensus among the plantation folk seems to be that the death is either justifiable homicide or unintentional manslaughter, no action is taken against Big Sue.

Then, after the burial, the "digression" is linked thematically and dramatically with the main action (April's story) when Zeda, Sherry's mother, slips into April's house while he is sleeping and lays

Leah's winding sheet across the foot of his bed—thereby "conjuring" him. Maum Hannah comes immediately and warns April not to burn the sheet since burning only intensifies the efficacy of the charm. But, proud and self-reliant as ever, April refuses to listen and tosses the sheet into the coals where it is scorched. In such an action, April exemplifies his impiety or hubris; he refuses not only to fear the forces of the unknown but also to respect the advice of his elder—the matriarchal Maum Hannah. He is so self-assured, so arrogant, that he refuses to submit to the powers of the supernatural or to heed traditional wisdom. Since he is a man who sets himself above God and community, he is, therefore, ripe for doom.

His "nemesis" begins to take definite form almost immediately thereafter, and Mrs. Peterkin begins to narrow the focus so subtly that the attention of the reader is finally centered like a spotlight on the foreman's powerful legs. After Leah's death, for example, April is lonely and is forever pacing about the plantation. There are those "choral" voices among the members of the community which prophesy that he will "walk himself to death," and the entire plantation population immediately sees the connection between his new restlessness and the conjured death sheet. His feet, they say, will "never rest again in this world, or in the other, unless [he makes] a change in his ways."

Joy, another instrument of April's doom, takes advantage of his restlessness when she accosts him on one of his walks to invite him to the house, ostensibly to see her mother, Big Sue. From that time on, the relationship between the two becomes more intimate, and eventually Breeze overhears April's marriage proposal to Joy. The scene—though somewhat awkwardly arranged in order to provide for a consistent point of view—foreshadows the tragic end of the marriage. April, the middle-aged man who has always had his pick of the plantation women, is filled with desire for the young girl; but he does not suspect that she is pregnant by his archrival—the man who will replace him as foreman—or that she is prepared to use him as a solution to her predicament. As he bends forward, she leans back, smiles to lure him on, and yet instinctively withdraws from his affection. Of course the irony is doubled because April himself has driven Joy to such deceitful measures by unfairly banishing Sherry from the plantation before she can tell the young man of her plight.

The next day April and Joy elope; and Big Sue, who is pleased at Joy's "triumph" without knowing its full implications, expresses her delight in statements which are classically ironic in light of later developments. "April was born fo' luck," she says. "E ever did git de best o' ev'yt'ing on dis plantation." The next hint of nemesis comes when a thunderbolt strikes the pinetree by April's house. The equation of the tall pine and April is one that the members of the community immediately acknowledge, and everyone suggests that April has angered God; but, like Oedipus, the foreman remains defiant in the face of unmistakable signs, and laughs at the superstitions of the chorus around him.

Joy, however, is so frightened that she delivers her child—so early that even April cannot fail to realize the truth. Thus the thunderbolt is something more than a warning; it is the cause of the first in a series of public humiliations that come to the proud man. After he fully understands what Joy has done to him, he looks at his young wife in her bed, snarls "bitch," and stalks from the room. Later Zeda, Sherry's mother, confronts April and gloats over what has happened. In a fine example of "anagnorisis," Zeda tells him that Sherry is the father of Joy's child, that the newborn infant is, therefore, not only her grandchild but also April's since he is Sherry's father. The irony here is exquisite, for April's own son—the progeny of his masculine pride—has been the chief cause of his public disgrace—has, in fact, slept with his own father's wife.

Before Zeda's onslaught, April remains surly and aloof; and once again the curse falls on him, this time from Zeda's lips: "You neck is stiff, enty! So's my own. An' I hope a misery'll gnaw you' heart in two. I hope you'll die of thirst an hunger. I hope ev'y yard-chile you had by Leah'll perish. I hope you' feet'll rot."[7] The curse here is traditional in form and has its origins in Classical as well as in Biblical lore. Not only does Zeda call down all manner of physical calamity on April, but she also invokes disaster on his "house"—the "yard-children" who legitimately bear his name (as opposed to "woods-colts" like Sherry). The repetition of the curse on his feet is ominous, but April still will not take heed.

And, in the next chapter, the reader sees what seems to be the first signs of the spell's efficacy. April's feet, for some reason, begin to trouble him; and some "choral" discussion occurs among the plantation folk as to whether or not the curse is having its effect. Uncle Bill speculates that it might be chilblain or ground-itch (thus providing an alternative explanation more satisfying to the skeptical reader), but the old man reaches no definite conclusions himself.

Here again Mrs. Peterkin is treading that thin line between the
natural and the supernatural, and she once again refuses to make a
final commitment, despite the circumstances of the story that seem
to indicate a stronger predisposition for the supernatural than she
had evinced in *Green Thursday*.

Whatever the explanation for April's affliction, he has not relented in his contention that spirits and conjures cannot hurt him;
and he refuses for awhile to accept a charm which Joy brings to him.
Then, partly out of a desire to please his young wife, whom he has
forgiven, and partly, perhaps, because he is beginning to have
doubts, he accepts a cloth bag to put around his neck. After it fails to
bring immediate relief, however, he tosses it into the fire. Once
again he has, according to superstition, done the worst possible
thing, and his feet immediately worsen. He refuses to send for a
white doctor; he asks instead that Maum Hannah be called, thus
humbling himself before the woman whose advice he has earlier
scorned. She comes to his aid, but her remedies are to no avail.

The moment April becomes aware of the hopelessness of his case
is one of extreme pathos. As he is sitting by the fire talking to Uncle
Bill, a coal suddenly pops onto the hearth and comes to rest between his feet. The coal is "red, bright, like a dare"; and April,
lifting his feet, places his heel on the coal. Then he lifts his foot again
and stares at Uncle Bill in horror; there is no feeling, for the foot is
utterly numb. After he quickly picks up the coal in his hands only to
drop it, he no longer doubts his fate. He has come to a moment of
dreadful defeat, and the defiant spirit that has driven him all his
years fails for the first time to bolster his self-control. The proud
man—who has, through strength of body and will, always mastered
himself, those around him, and the very elements themselves as
foreman of the plantation—suddenly loses control. With tears
streaming down his cheeks, he cries aloud that he has given out,
that he cannot go on any longer; and, when Joy enters the room, he
weeps on her breast. This cry is an essential element of tragedy—
the hero's admission of his own finiteness in the face of the over-
whelming forces that are arrayed against him.

The scene which follows, another treatment of Mrs. Peterkin's
own experience with her foreman, is perhaps the most terrifying in
the book; and she renders it in agonizing detail, building to the
horrifying climax with the infinite patience and skill of a Gothic
novelist. Uncle Bill, worried about April's deteriorating condition,

takes matters into his own hands and brings some of the "white
man's medicine," which he says will help. The old man and Joy heat
water, fill a tub, pour in the white liquid, and put April's feet into
the solution to soak. After a while, when April is ready to go to bed,
Joy kneels down to wipe the feet, suddenly recoils in horror, and
cries "Great Gawd, what has you done, Uncle Bill?" In a fine touch,
April ironically believes something is wrong with Joy; and, when she
tries to stand up and staggers, he scolds her: "Don' try fo stan' up.
You might fall. None o' we ain' able to ketch you if you do. You
haffer take care o' you' se'f now. I ain' able fo' look atter you'."[8]

Gradually Breeze (through whose eyes the scene is viewed) and
April realize that Joy's strange behavior has been caused by April's
condition rather than by her own, and the true horror of what has
happened is revealed:

> Breeze's eyes followed Joy's to the tub. He stared too. He saw what made
> her teeth click together—
> April's toes.
> They had come loose from his feet, and floated around in the tub. In the
> clear warm water, sharp-flavored with the strong white medicine. Breeze
> felt dazed. His head was queer. The room, the walls began to move around
> and wave up and down.
> When April saw the toes he began to laugh. An ugly, croaking, high-
> pitched laugh that chilled Breeze's blood, and made the water swish in the
> tub.
> The toes, all loose, free from the feet, swam around swiftly and circled
> and danced. One big toe slid next to a little one and stopped!
> April half-rose to his feet and shouted:
> "Look! My Gawd! Is you ever see sich a t'ing in you' life? My toes is come
> off. Dey runs by deyse'f! Fo' Gawd's sake!"
> His reddened eyes shone. He tried to step. Then he sat down clumsily.
> Heavily. He leaned forward, spellbound, whispering horrified words.
> Breeze shook with terror, for April's words were as strange as the toes
> jumbled together. He glared at Breeze, then at Uncle Bill. "Yunnuh hurry
> up! Hurry up!" he yelled fiercely, getting up on his feet again. "Do somet'-
> ing! Quick! My toes is off!"
> He tottered, for the bottom of the tub was slippery footing for his broken
> feet, and with a crumple he fell forward on the floor.[9]

In this scene, April's "spiritual" fall is made concrete in explicit and
literal terms by his physical one. Indeed, the incident is something

of a telescoped version of the entire action. After imperiously warning Joy not to risk a fall, he himself—in a desperate attempt to
frustrate the fate that has overtaken him—stands up, shouts orders,
and topples to the floor. From that time forward, Joy must take care
of him; and the words he has scolded her with take on an exquisite
irony.

The terror Breeze feels in this scene is the terror of the audience
that has witnessed a tragedy. Removed from the mind of the protagonist and yet involved to a degree in the events that lead to his
triumph, Breeze sees in the fall of April the fall of man and his own
impending doom. When April tries to hold a mirror in order to look
at his feet, Breeze must steady his father's trembling hand, but the
boy too becomes frightened, and April's horror makes "Breeze's
own blood freeze."

And later, when Breeze is in church and hears the story of Jonah,
". . . he shuddered from head to foot with horror and pity for poor
Jonah. God seemed as cruel and awful as the Devil. Between the
two, there was small chance of any safety. Poor Jonah! Poor April!
Poor Breeze."[10] The phrase "horror and pity" may be merely coin-
cidental, but it suggests a literary sophistication on Mrs. Peterkin's
part that even her most ardent supporters during the earlier years
never gave her credit for. For Breeze feels the emotions which
Aristotle attributes to the audience of tragedy; and, in the applica-
tion Breeze makes to himself, something akin to catharsis appears.
He easily sees in the story of Jonah implications that are first applicable to April's fate, and then he realizes that he himself is a potential
victim of the same power. Shortly before April dies, Breeze begins
"to seek" in an effort to avoid the same downfall; but the significance of his new piety is undercut to some extent by his conduct
with Emma, a girl his own age, to whom he boasts of his prowess
and lack of fear. The scene ends with Emma running away, taunting
Breeze about his religion. Breeze, forgetting his fear of God, exults
in his manhood—his strong legs that have been the downfall of his
father. Thus there is still pride to be purged.

In the meantime, April's humiliation is intensified by the fact that
in a time of crisis—the boll weevils are destroying the cotton—the
people on the plantation no longer look to him for help but decide
instead to ask Sherry to return and take over the duties of foreman.
It was April, of course, who drove Sherry from the plantation at a
time when the proud foreman was master of the community; there-

fore, Sherry's triumphal return is a harsh rebuke. The young man is met on the dock by cheering well-wishers, one of whom is Joy. Though Sherry has married in the North, he has left his wife behind; and he and Joy hold a brief conversation that suggests their earlier intimacy may be revived.

Later, when April returns from the hospital after the amputation of his legs, Sherry carries him off the boat; and April's body is "not much longer than Joy's baby now." With the description of April's emaciated body, the reader is reminded that only a few months earlier April has defeated in battle the man who now bears him in his arms as he would a frail child. April is glad to be back, and he expresses his satisfaction that Sherry has been made foreman—an act of reconciliation that elicits a generous remark from the younger man to the effect that he will never be as good a foreman as April was. Then, after being taken to his cabin, April breaks into tears.

Shortly thereafter the full implications of his altered community status begin to weigh on him as, lying flat on his back, he hears Sherry operating "the poison machine" used to rid the cotton fields of boll weevils. But fate has not quite finished with him; the most exquisite punishment is yet to come—the blow which finally destroys him. Joy, whose renewed interest in Sherry has been obvious from the moment he returns, begins to spend her evenings away from the house. At first, April accepts this conduct as natural and says nothing; but, when he learns one stormy night the true meaning of her nocturnal visits, the knowledge is too much for him to bear. Joy returns late; and April, who has been disturbed by the sounds of the storm, hears her enter. Crawling out of bed and moving on his arms, he creeps across the floor and listens at the door to her room. When what he hears convinces him that she is with Sherry, "Suddenly, something inside him seemed to break. Something in his head or his breast. With a yell he beat on the door, and tried to break it down. Then he lost his balance and fell back on the floor where he lay and raved and cursed himself and Joy and God."[11]

Like Job, he now has had to bear all things; but, unlike Job, he curses God. After a few days he dies. The final knowledge—that he has been cuckolded in his own house by his own son—breaks his already tortured spirit; and he surrenders to the fever that has racked his body. That Sherry is the instrument of his ultimate defeat is ironically fitting; but, since the punishment April bears is too much for the sins he has committed, he, like Oedipus, moves to tears those who view his end.

His death, however, is not without the dignity that befits a tragic hero. Instead of sinking into a delirium and then to unconsciousness, he comes to his senses just before the end and speaks to Uncle Bill, who is by his bedside. First he tells the old man that he is unafraid; indeed, he welcomes death as a relief from his afflictions. Then he asks one final favor, or rather charges Uncle Bill with one final duty; and, in doing so, April reveals that he is still something of the man he once was:

"Uncle—" April's breath stifled, his eyes widened with the strain, but he forced his lips to twist out the words he wanted to say.

"Bury me in a man-size box—You un'erstan'?—A man—size—box— I—been—six—feet—fo'—Uncle— Six feet—fo'!"

The blaze in his eyes fell back, cold, dim. A long shudder swept over him. The tide had turned.[12]

IV   In Summary

While *Black April* is by no means a perfect novel, it may be Mrs. Peterkin's most powerful work of fiction. To be sure, the plot is essentially episodic, with occasional pauses in the action for sociological catalogues; yet Mrs. Peterkin clearly learns something about rendering a scene in the writing of this book. She allows herself the leisurely pace to develop relationships slowly and thoroughly through the use of extended dialogue and longer descriptive passages. And her style is more complex than in *Green Thursday*. The use of dialect is essentially the same—still suggestive rather than imitative—but the relatively sophisticated diction and syntax of the narrative and descriptive passages are appropriate to the tragic implications of April's story.

Again, as suggested earlier, the critics were enthusiastic in their reception of this novel. Indeed their appraisal of her intentions and achievement were, in many cases, the most accurate evaluation she would receive during her lifetime. Certainly the novel prepared the stage for her next performance, when she was to outdo herself one more time and win a Pulitzer Prize.

CHAPTER 4

The Triumph of Comedy

IF *Black April* is a tragedy with a classic action, then *Scarlet Sister
Mary* is just as surely a classic comedy and in this regard it is
interesting to note Northrop Frye's discussion of Aristophanes. In
the works of this Greek playwright, says Frye, a central figure usually

constructs his (or her) own society. . . driving away all the people who
come to prevent or exploit him; and [he] eventually achieves a heroic
triumph, complete with mistresses, in which he is sometimes assigned the
honors of a reborn god. We notice that just as there is the catharsis of pity
and fear in tragedy, so is there the catharsis of the corresponding comic
emotions, sympathy and ridicule, in Old Comedy. The comic hero achieves
his triumph whether what he has done is sensible or silly, honest or ras-
cally.[1]

A reading of *Scarlet Sister Mary* reveals a number of remarkable
parallels to the plot Frye outlines. This novel, Mrs. Peterkin's third
book of fiction, chronicles the life of a black plantation woman, Mary
Pinesett, from the point in her life when she is just coming to
womanhood until the moment in early middle age when she renounces a life of illicit lovers and illegitimate children. She is received back into the bosom of the church, but not until she has
shamed her self-righteous enemies and retained something of her
good-hearted sensuality. Thus in many ways Frye's typical description is as applicable to Mrs. Peterkin's novel as it is to the works of
Aristophanes; and it provides the reader with a means of analyzing
the plot structure of Mrs. Peterkin's narrative and of understanding
the relationship of its essential parts. In the first part of the book,
Mary does indeed "construct her own society" after deliberately
choosing ostracism from the one into which she was born. When she
dances at her wedding party and begins to show signs of pregnancy

thereafter, she is excommunicated by the church and relegated to the category of exiled sinner. Her response to this action is to establish her own moral code—to take her pleasure and derive her livelihood from whatever men are available, and never to commit herself emotionally to any of them, lest they betray her. With this code she is the scandal of the plantation and the terror of every insecure wife. Because of her charm and her strength, however, no one is able to subdue her. One rival—Cinder—steals her husband, but Mary survives the blow; and, when the homewrecker is in turn discarded, Mary chides her for her inability to recover and proves her own superiority of character. While the deacons denounce Mary, she cajoles the most vociferous among them to do manual labor for her that would properly fall to a husband. When Maum Hannah chides her for living in sin outside the salvation of the church, she asserts that she will trick the devil yet and be reinstated. By the end of the novel, she has done just that. And the nine men who are the fathers of her many children—though the men are happy and satisfied in her company—never possess her completely. Even the husband whom she married for love at the age of fifteen is turned from her door when he returns, a supplicant, many years later. In summary, she prevails over all men and circumstances.

Frye's reference to the "reborn god" is interesting in the light of Mary's ultimate return to the church. Because she has been so sinful, the deacons finally decide that the first baptism was not efficacious enough and insist that she be "reborn" a second time. Having observed this ritual, she is again one of the saved; and, as such, she is reintegrated both spiritually and socially into the community. As final evidence of her independence, however, she retains her "conjure bag," which she believes has attracted her many lovers; for she is not ready to give up her old ways completely. Thus, as Frye suggests about Aristophanes' characters, Mary's triumph is inevitable despite her years of misconduct. To be sure, sympathy outweighs ridicule in this particular narrative; but both emotions are evoked. Indeed, the humorous scenes in *Scarlet Sister Mary* are among the best in modern Southern literature.

I *Theme, Conflict, Point of View*

Although *Scarlet Sister Mary* is about Gullahs, their customs, and their beliefs, it presents a vision of life that is quite different in a number of significant ways from that presented in *Black April* or in *Green Thursday*.

Scarlet Sister Mary is concerned primarily with the conflict between church doctrine and natural instinct. This theme is of course important in *Green Thursday*, but in *Scarlet Sister Mary* the emphasis is on the relationship of the central character to the community; in *Green Thursday*, the relationship of Killdee to his fellow Gullahs is of minor importance except in one story, "Mount Pleasant."

Indeed, the title *Scarlet Sister Mary* itself suggests the nature of the conflict. "Mary" has connotations that are Christian and at the same time secular since the name is not only that of the mother of Christ but also the most common of all feminine names; therefore, its use is, in a sense, another way of saying "Everywoman." "Sister" is also the "title" given to all women accepted into the congregation of the black church, and to be called "Sister" is to be recognized as among those purified by baptism and therefore heavenbound. "Scarlet," on the other hand, is traditionally the color of venial sin, and more explicitly of sexual sin, not only in such sophisticated literary works as Hawthorne's *The Scarlet Letter* but also in the simple folklore of the Gullah black.

To be "Scarlet Sister Mary," therefore, is to be a woman torn between good and evil, one whose desire for spiritual salvation is counterbalanced by her natural physical instinct to love and be loved regardless of the moral strictures laid down by the primitive Christian Church. Such is the conflict within Mrs. Peterkin's heroine; and, while the life-struggle is an important factor in Mary's life—as it is in the lives of all the characters the author depicts—it is no more than an interesting counterpoint to the main theme in this work.

II *The Narrative*

The narrative begins with a three page chapter that describes in general terms the locale, the people, and something of their historical background. This brief discourse serves the same purpose as the first two-thirds of *Black April*, and the economy Mrs. Peterkin exemplifies is evidence of her growing skill as a craftsman. For the first time she defines the blacks as "Gullahs," differentiating them from the Guineas and the Dinkas. She also gives a brief history of the plantation system from ante-bellum days to a time beyond Reconstruction when the white man abandons the "Big House" and leaves the land and its problems to the blacks. This change after the Civil War is as far as she will go, however, in defining the relation-

ship between the whites and the blacks. As in previous works, she
pictures the modern plantation life of her characters as isolated from
the mainstream of American life to such an extent that social, political, and economic trends leave it relatively untouched. Only nature
has its effect, and even nature cannot destroy or erode the essence
of the plantation community.[2]

As in Mrs. Peterkin's earlier fiction, the plot covers a number of
years in the life of Mary, the main character. The novel begins with
a brief summary of her early youth, including her baptism; and the
narrative then focuses on her wedding day at the age of fifteen when
her pregnancy is discovered and her expulsion from the church is
assured. The novel ends with her rebaptism after the death of her
first child, Unex, and after a span of over twenty years during which
she has borne nine children, eight of them out of wedlock. The
circular movement of the narrative indicates Mrs. Peterkin's new
concern for tight structure and artistic unity, for the final outcome of
the action is incipient in the opening scene. Unex, the unborn child
and an incarnation of Mary's "scarlet sin," will, through his death,
bring about her repentance, cleanse her, and prepare her for rebaptism into the church from which she was expelled at his birth.

Vague though the Christian mythological implications of such a
narrative may be, the theological implications are specifically introduced at the outset and form an integral part of the theme. Mary's
"seeking" at the age of twelve; her dream of the "heavenly" White
House with the anthropomorphic God who tenders His forgiveness;
her renunciation of dancing, "reel songs," and other sinful
occupations—all of these introduce the central conflict between
natural and religious impulses that is to divide not only the black
community but also the heart of Sister Mary.

That division is not long in revealing itself. She is courted by
brothers, June and July, who—though they are twins—are unlike in
almost every significant respect. June, who is "short, big-chested,
heavy, slow," is the Good Angel and represents the virtues of loy-
alty, diligence, and respectability. Though he is not a church
member (Mrs. Peterkin does not overstate the contrast), he is the
choice of stepmother Maum Hannah and her crippled son, Budda
Ben. On the other hand, July,—tall, lean, quick-spoken—is described as "a wicked sinner, a crap-shooter, a poker-player, a gam-
bler, a dancer who sang reels, and carried his 'box' (guitar)

everywhere he went playing wicked tunes for the sinners to dance by at birth-night suppers and parties and playing on Saturday afternoon at the crossroads store for the boys and men who loafed there when the week's work was over."[3]

July is the Bad Angel; and, though Mary is fond of June, she chooses July. With this choice, her alienation from the religious community is assured; indeed, it is foretold by Maum Hannah after she discovers that the young bride is pregnant.

The life Mary will lead is clearly foreshadowed when July borrows money from June and buys her as a wedding present a pair of gold earrings wrapped in a scarlet handkerchief. These two objects appeal to her love of beauty and pleasure, and, as symbols, they pervade the entire narrative. Indeed, in the end, when she repents of her sins, she still refuses to discard her earrings or her conjure bag—a love charm—and adds a note of ambiguity to her second redemption.

After the wedding ceremony, July takes Mary to the tavern named "Foolishness" where she sees more sinners bound for hell—singing, dancing, drinking. The description is rich with sensual imagery; and in the midst of ecstatic dancers, flowing wine, and steaming heaps of food is the figure of Cinder, whose name suggests both spent passion and the ashes of hell. Mrs. Peterkin's description of Cinder defines her symbolic role in the action:

> She was ugly and black and skinny, but she knew how to snatch men away from their women as brazenly as foxes snatch hens from their mates in the fig trees. July was so taken up with showing off some of the new steps he had learned away from home, he could not see how Cinder's eyes shone with wickedness, or how sharp her white teeth showed between her thin black lips. With every heart-beat, Mary's anger and jealousy grew,[4]

Cinder, as seen through the eyes of Mary, is the embodiment of animal passion—the fox—and Mary sees immediately that this quality dominates July. If she is to hold him, she will have to compete with Cinder; but such a course means the flouting of her religious vows. She considers the alternatives, when June asks her to dance:

> She could feel her body yielding while the two minds inside her considered what was best to do. One mind said, "No," and the other mind

answered, "You are the best dancer here. Show the people that Cinder has
no time with you," and before she knew it, she heard her lips saying:
    "Get de box, June, and play me a tune. I rather dance by myself out here
in de yard."[5]

The flames from the bonfire, a threat of hell, leap higher as Mary
begins her dance; and outside, in the black night, she is an isolated
figure close to the heart of nature. The earth rocks, the trees sway,
and the music grows wilder. Suddenly July is there, he looks at her
with steady eyes, and he is ready at last to take her home. She has
made her choice, has triumphed over Cinder, and for the moment is
happy.
    Soon thereafter, however, Mary is dismissed from the church, as
Maum Hannah has predicted; but, as long as her husband is faithful,
she is satisfied with the choice she has made. July, however, proves
to be a poor man for doing things around the house; and June bears
much of his brother's work burden, including the killing of the hogs.
Squeamishness is the reason July will not butcher the animals which
he has earlier marked as his own by slashing their ears. His reluctance suggests that he is less a man than Mary realizes; for, in this
primitive agrarian community in which death is the sine qua non of
life, both men and women learn as part of their everyday activity to
slaughter hogs, wring the necks of chickens, and shoot squirrels. No
man worthy of the name would beg another to perform such duties
for him any more than he would wish another man to support his
family. Mary soon discovers that July is no more interested in assuming his responsibilities toward her than he is in taking care of his
own livestock.
    With disaster just around the corner, Mary begins to experience
the sense of loss that is an inevitable result of isolation from one's
heritage and community. The first acute awareness of this loss
comes in Chapter VII, which contains a description of Christmas-
time on the plantation that begins with the folk games of the children, ends with the "all-night watch meeting" at Maum Hannah's
on Christmas Eve, and climaxes with the reading of the Nativity
story and an unbearable explosion of joy at the stroke of midnight.
Mary's isolation is emphasized in concrete terms when she is forced
to remain in the back of the church with the "sinners" and to hear
the story of Christ's birth as she sits in the darkness and cold—away
from the stove that provides warmth and light at the front. While

she suffers this humiliation with a sense of longing, July is rolling
dice with the men.

Once again parallels to the gospel suggest themselves. Mary,
who, like her namesake, is carrying a child on Christmas Eve, listens to the shouts of joy from the congregation as the good news is
told while July is "casting lots" elsewhere. Thus in this one scene
the major conflict is once again stated, and its end—the death of the
firstborn child Unex and Mary's "redemption"—is obliquely
foreshadowed. The Christmas scene, however, does more than simply underline the central theme of the narrative. It also serves as a
dramatic contrast to the lonely months that follow when Mary, left
alone in her cabin by July, awaits without the companionship of the
"sisters" the birth of her child. This contrast between community
social life and the isolation of the sinner is almost Augustinian in its
implications. The folk games, the fireworks—these activities derive
from the religious significance of the holiday and are properly the
celebrations of the "saved." Sinners are allowed limited participa-
tion, but they are clearly outside the circle of love—both God's and
the community's.

In Chapter VIII, Mary begins her long battle to hold July, a battle
which ends in his defection to Cinder. Except for the birth of Unex,
which occurs in the middle of a dusty road (hence the name "Unexpected"), Mary's life is dull and uneventful. She has a few visitors
and is happy enough while tending to her newborn child, but her
longing for July and her growing hatred of Cinder become more
obsessive as the tedious days go by. In Chapter IX, Cinder comes to
visit Mary; and her character is defined more fully. Such definition
is important, not only to provide a contrast with Mary, who is only
partly the creature of passion, but also to delineate in more detail
July's inherent weakness since this woman embodies the qualities
he most admires. The description of Cinder reintroduces some of
the symbols already defined in relation to Mary, and their total
significance is further developed:

She had a string of red beads around her neck, gold earrings in her ears, and
a gold ring on one finger. In spite of the scent of cooking food, the whole
room smelled sweet from something about her; not Hoyt's German Cologne
or essence of lemon or any of the perfumes Mary knew, but a strange new
scent, that was delicate as the breath of crabapple blossoms. Just as likely as
not it came from some new charm Cinder got yonder in town to put a spell

on the men here. She always knew some way to make the men take to her, although she was skinny and dry, and had a fox chin and squirrel teeth and a sly stepping walk like a cat.[6]

The earrings and beads, gold and red, are the colors of greed and passion; and they recall to the reader the earrings and the red bandanna that July had brought Mary as a wedding gift. The irony of that gift is now apparent; these gifts represent the qualities that July has brought to their marriage, and they are the qualities that ultimately lead to its dissolution, since Cinder lures July away with golden earrings and red beads. Her essential animality is revealed in the final sequence when she is described as a fox, a squirrel, and a cat—the first animal is a crafty robber; the second, a thief; and the third, a predator.

Cinder greets Mary with arrogance; and, when she smells a 'possum cooking, she demands some of the meat—a queen in her rival's kitchen. Her sensuality makes her brazen and self-indulgent; and Mary, whose sensuality is balanced by some sense of propriety, is forced to serve Cinder. However, the wily interloper is not invincible; like all sinners she is helpless before the power of God. This power suddenly and significantly manifests itself in a traditional way. "A sudden flash of lightning made Cinder jump, and Mary looked straight at her mouth. 'I'd be afraid so much gold and silver would draw lightnin',' she remarked."

This use by Mary of folklore is an indication of the artistic control Mrs. Peterkin had gained over her subject matter since the writing of *Black April*. Mary uses the superstition as a threat to hurl at Cinder, a threat in which her own moral conflict is embodied. Also, the storm, which grows in intensity throughout the scene, acts as an objectification of the intensifying hatred that the two rivals feel for each other.

The scene ends with the entrance of July who, when he sees Cinder arrayed in all of her cheap trappings, tracks mud on his own hearth, a gesture with obvious implications. Cinder—once again described as foxlike—turns her charms on him and the two carry on a shameless flirtation as if Mary and the child were not even present. Later that evening July leaves without any explanation; and, when he returns, Mary smells the scent of Cinder's new perfume. The storm has subsided, the voice of God is stilled, and the musky odor of sensuality signals Cinder's triumph. Mary's explanation for July's behavior both salves her wounded pride and assigns greater malignancy to Cinder, for she concludes that July has been "conjured." As if to confirm her worst suspicions, he leaves her to take a short trip; and as a result, Mary goes to Daddy Cudjoe for help and finds out that Cinder has procured a love charm herself in order to win July. Daddy, therefore, must devise a charm to counteract his own magic—which he did not realize Cinder was planning to use on July. The old man gives Mary some good advice as he prepares the concoction—a mixture of blood, skin, toenail, hair, and root. He suggests that she might think about finding someone else to love; and, from the way he talks, he seems to understand that July is already under Cinder's spell and that he will not return from his excursion. As Mary is about to leave, Daddy gives her a parting word of wisdom which epitomizes the paradox of human love; he tells her that it can never be imprisoned but must remain free and is, therefore, liable to loss.

And July does not return to Mary after the excursion, but the conjure bag she gets from Daddy Cudjoe is not wasted. June continues to attend Mary in his brother's absence; but discouraged because she seems beyond his reach, he finally announces that he too is leaving the plantation. Mary, suddenly realizing how much she depends on him, takes down the love charm from the mantle and contrives to touch him with it. At the same time, she confesses how fond she is of him; and he agrees to stay. Mary believes the conjure bag has worked its magic, but the touch of her hand and her promise of an old desire's fulfillment are explanation enough for June's behavior.

Once again for Mary the mystery of sexual attraction needs supernatural explanation. That June's passion is no more than sexual is confirmed in the succeeding paragraphs in which an equation is set up between June and the rooster in the barnyard. The rooster tricks the hens into coming to his side by pretending to have found some tasty morsel, and June begins to flatter Mary by praising her beauty and by telling her how much he is infatuated by her. Regardless of the fact that she, herself, recognizes the evidence of masculine deceit in man and rooster, she, like the hens, is helplessly caught in the wave of her own physical desire; and the scene closes with Mary breathless and speechless because of June's blandishments.

Before she accepts June as a lover, she goes to meeting, partially out of loneliness and partially to ask God to return her husband. Once again, her dilemma is revealed. She sits in the back of the room with the sinners, far away from the fire, the kerosene lamp, and the Bible—all of which symbolize the light of the true faith. When Maum Hannah invites her to move to the front, she refuses, citing as her reason the warmth of the fire, which would give the baby a cold. In reality, however, she prefers her seat near the door so that she can see if July returns. Since she is still drawn to the world of outer darkness, she chooses isolation with the sinners though she yearns to be at one with the congregation. "Just inside the door" is the perfect description of her relationship to the Christian community.

As the days pass, Mary becomes more and more despondent; and she finally tells Budda Ben, who has come to visit her, that she wishes she were dead. The crippled man, whose sorrows have been greater than hers, rebukes her sternly, telling her she cannot choose the time of her death but must look to the future. She takes herself too seriously, he says; she is not the first to be tricked by a man nor will she be the last. When he ends his lecture with some advice about how to smoke, his words are obviously as applicable to her problem with July as to his: he stresses discipline, patience, and slow enjoyment. After this talk, Mary thinks about what Budda Ben has told her and resolves to follow his advice. This resolution is concretely objectified in the scene that follows, and her new attitude results in the "conjuring" of June.

Mary's acceptance of June, which results in the birth of a second child a year later, is a significant thematic development in the novel since it marks the end of Mary's enslavement to July and the beginning of a new attitude toward love and life in general—an attitude which increases her alienation from the church community. She still longs to be a part of the religious life of the congregation, but she no longer seems to resent the disapproval of the faithful. She does not even expect to find love since she realizes that, as far as men are concerned, "not one of them is worth a drop of water that drains out of a woman's eyes."

Mary, hardened toward religion and love, paradoxically becomes more compassionate toward others and even feels sorry for Cinder who, she now believes, is simply another victim of July's diabolical ways. Thus she feels a kind of sisterly affection for all women, as embodied in her former rival; and she even visits Cinder in the broken-down shack where July has left her. Cinder continues to grieve for him, but Mary is stronger. As both Daddy Cudjoe and

Budda Ben have told her, there are plenty of other men to be found; and, though she is no longer a victim of love and though her view of men is a jaded one, she by no means forsakes their company. Instead, she seeks it more than ever, both because men give her pleasure and because they provide her with the necessities of life. After June, she has a series of lovers who are nameless and faceless to the reader and who become the various fathers of her seven additional children.

Despite Mary's sympathy with the plight of women and her contempt for men, she has to struggle with her own sex for the enjoyment and the comfort that men provide. In this respect, she is a "man's woman," despite her inherent distrust of men; and her paradoxical nature reminds one of Chaucer's Wife of Bath: Mary is sexually demanding, but she will never become a slave to men; she chooses to dominate them. She is frank in admitting her vices, yet she does not seem less attractive because of them. She is an affront to respectability, and yet she commands the respect and affection of respectable people.

Unlike the Wife of Bath, of course, Mary does not enter the church before all others do. In fact, she grieves for the loss of her place within the Christian community. She regards the faithful for what they are—sheep who cling together because they haven't the strength to be independent; and she also sees in the case of Budda Ben—who is turned out of the church for cursing cruel and disrespectful children—how unjust the self-righteous deacons can be about the sins of others. Yet Mary is still religious; she looks for God in nature, believes in punishment for sin and reward for virtue, and even goes to see the motion picture of Hell out of a sense of duty as well as curiosity. She is simply unwilling to surrender her way of life in order to accept the church's discipline. The conflict, then, is essentially the same; but her attitude toward it is different. Where once she was idealistic about both the church and love, her viewpoint is now more cynical—indeed more realistic.

Thus far in the novel, Mrs. Peterkin has employed the scenic technique; she has carefully developed Mary's character and moral dilemma with a series of concrete scenes which take place over a relatively short span in her life. Once the author has thoroughly defined Mary's fall from innocence into disillusionment, however, she switches to the panoramic for a summary of the fifteen years that intervene between the time she bears June's child (Seraphine) at the

beginning of Chapter XVII and the time in the opening scenes of
Chapter XVIII when she is on her way to persuade Andrew to make
a pair of crutches for Keepsie, her youngest son. This chapter begins
with the change to the panoramic view which is dictated by the
necessity to bridge the years between Mary's great spiritual disillusionment and her ultimate return to the church. The thematic significance of the intervening years is trivial, but the events illustrate
the profound effect that Mary's newly acquired cynicism has had on
her beliefs and conduct. A series of men provide a sufficient example, but that they are mentioned casually in summary and not by
name is singularly appropriate since they mean nothing individually
to the "scarlet sister."

After the panorama of fifteen years, Mrs. Peterkin returns to the
scenic technique to describe Budda Ben's expulsion from the congregation for cursing. This incident serves as a significant parallel to
the central action since Budda Ben is to some extent a victim of the
self-righteous church community, just as Mary is; and he is particularly a victim of the powerful and pietistic Andrew, whose cruel,
brattish children have goaded the crippled little man into an un-
Christian rage. Andrew, of course, is a former suitor of Mary's; and
he is hardest on her when her name comes up for discussion among
the deacons.

Like Mary, Budda Ben is eventually reintegrated into the church
community—indeed, several times before the novel ends; but the
painful humiliation he suffers is analogous to that which Mary has
suffered. Moreover her attitude toward his excommunication is a
good indication of her adjustment to her own years of isolation. For
her, resolution has hardened into a cynical veneer that almost covers her essential warmth and compassion. When she speaks to Ben,
she does not comfort him with sympathetic words; she berates him
for his lack of control. Her tone of voice, in fact, is reminiscent of
Ben's own earlier speech in which he "talked sense" to her about
July's departure. There is in Mary's argument, however, something
more—a pragmatic realism born of bitter experience and struggle.
Just as she can now regard men with detached objectivity, so can
she dispassionately examine the church; and her advice to Ben,
cynical though it may sound to him, is simply the cold, hard truth:
" 'You's a fallen member now, but don' fret about it. Abusin de
deacons ain' gwine put you back whe you was. Do keep quiet. When

you git ready, you can pray an' seek an' find peace an' jine de church again'."7

This speech suggests what is in Mary's own mind and foreshadows, to some extent, the ending of the book. Like many a sinner, she holds to the thought that ultimate salvation is still a possibility. St. Augustine, writing about his early years, recalls praying for chastity, yet hoping all the while that God would postpone the answering of his prayer until his passion was satisfied. Mary, then, is no better and no worse than that devout church father in his youth; and what she tells Budda Ben seems also to be true of herself.

When Maum Hannah sternly lectures her for being too hard on the poor man, Mary allows herself to be chastened, partly because she loves and respects Maum Hannah and partly because her hard, irreverent talk only reveals one side of her. At heart, she is frightened by Maum Hannah's warning of eternal damnation and by her prediction of impending catastrophe. Mary still longs for the innocence she has lost, as revealed by her special feeling for Unex, July's child (her only legitimate one), and by her protest to Maum Hannah that she is going to change and escape Satan's grasp.

Maum Hannah, however, is unconvinced. When she prophesies disaster, she cites the loss of one son's leg, the departure of Unex, and the failure of Mary's cotton crop as examples of God's judgment; and she warns that Mary's daughters will follow in her footsteps. This speech foreshadows two of the significant events that befall Mary before her conversion—her oldest daughter Seraphine's love affair and the death of Unex. Mary, though she loves Maum Hannah and believes abstractly in the church doctrine, cannot feel the immediacy of her danger or the imminence of the promised land: "For to save Mary's life she could not keep her mind fixed on the joys of Heaven, but sought her pleasure right here in this world, where pleasures are in such easy reach. She believed in God and Satan and Heaven and Hell too, and she had no doubt that sinners fed Hell's fires, but the rules of Heaven's Gate Church made the Christian life very difficult for a strong, healthy woman."8

Despite Budda Ben's tearful protest that she will be consorting with enemies, Mary goes to Andrew to ask the hard-headed deacon to make a pair of crutches for her child because Andrew is the best carpenter on the plantation; and the scene between the two reveals concretely both her vibrant sexuality and her essential

Christian goodness. On the surface, the scene may seem irrelevant
and anecdotal; but it is, in fact, a confrontation that reveals not only
the essential conflict between the natural and the spiritual, but also
the ambiguity of Mary's status as sinner in a church-oriented community. Both thematically and dramatically, then, this scene is
highly functional.

Mary's approach to Andrew is as deliberate as the stalk of a lioness
(or a vixen) and as skillful. Though she has "kept company" with him
in her youth—and though he of all deacons has been most severe in
his condemnation of her—she is confident that she can persuade
him to build the crutches for Keepsie, not because he is a Christian
and therefore charitable, but because he is a man and therefore
weak. Then, too, his studied indifference to her represents a challenge; and she concludes that such a stern, righteous life is unnatural, that "a little crooked walking might do him good." She
immediately flatters him by praising his upright propriety; and
then, when he protests that he too has troubles, she counters with
the oldest and most durable of feminine ploys—she invites him to
talk about himself, expertly leading him into a discussion of his
wife's inadequacies and their lack of rapport. When she sympathizes
with him, he begins to warm up to her: "You got sense, Si May-e,
sense like a man." When he attempts to change the subject, she
brings him back to his domestic difficulties and allows him to com-
plain at some length about his marital discord. After he has
finished, she speaks; and her words exemplify the wisdom she has
acquired in dealing with men. Instead of denouncing his wife Doll
(whom she despises) and siding with Andrew, thus putting him on
the defensive where his wife is concerned, she gives Doll her due
and states the complexity of the situation: " 'My first mind say, "Tell
Andrew to don' never fool wid Doll, not no more," but my second
mind say, "Tell Andrew fo Gawd's sake go hitch up a mule an' wagon
an' fetch Doll back home." ' "9

Andrew is completely confused by her advocacy of his cause and
by her careful sympathy for Doll. He finally pays her a compliment
that states the paradox of her position within the black community:
"Si May-e you's a good 'oman. You got a good heart, even if you is de
wickedest sinner Gawd ever made." In Andrew, the rigid orthodoxy
of the church again comes in direct conflict with the world of
human experience. Andrew recognizes, or thinks he recognizes, a
goodness in Mary that the theology of the church refuses to sanctify.

She is by definition a sinner; and no amount of goodness—i.e., kindness, sympathy, charitable deeds—can eradicate this unpleasant "truth."

The conflict is an ancient one dating back to the earliest days of Christianity when the question of faith versus good works was first debated. Beyond the boundaries of Blue Brook, the Protestant church of the 1920's was beginning to favor an answer that tended to minimize the orthodox "forms" of faith and to emphasize the more "humanitarian" virtues that Mary exemplifies; but Mrs. Peterkin makes no attempt to do more than present the paradox as it occurs to Andrew, who does not appear overly disturbed by it but seems to accept it as a logical tenet of his catechism.

Mary ends her "defense" of Doll by suggesting that Andrew apologize to her. When he protests that he is not at fault, she tells him that "It don' matter who done right or wrong. If you go humble like to Doll an' beg em pardon, it would do em an' you all-two good." The advice that Mary gives Andrew is not only psychologically but also theologically sound. Knowing that Doll is a spoiled, stubborn woman, Mary realizes that the easiest way to return to her good graces is by the path of humility. But Mary is also confronting the deacon with the spirit, if not the exact phrasing, of Christ's words in the Sermon on the Mount when He says, "Blessed are the peacemakers," "Agree with thine adversary quickly, whiles thou art in the way with him," or "And whosoever shall compel thee to go a mile, go with him twain."

It is significant that Andrew neither recognizes the true Christian spirit nor responds emotionally to its embodiment. In fact, he refuses to accept Mary's advice, despite her entreaties; and he closes the subject with the grim lament that women can no longer be ruled by a leather strap. Thus the "argument" is between the way of reconciliation and the way of might; and the sinner upholds the Christian position while the deacon advocates the use of brute force.

Following her conference with Andrew, Mary makes a rare visit to the church in order to take advantage of the instruction about "birthin' " offered by a social worker from the North. Because she has tarried too long with Andrew, she arrives after the instruction is over; but, since the ladies of the church have not left, what follows is a "hen-fight" both humorous and revealing. Doll, in particular, greets her with contempt; but Mary looks at the women, "some of them fat, some of them shriveled," and suddenly regains her confidence. She realizes that in contrast to them (and the attitudes they represent) she is "young, firm-bodied, a part of the fresh outside day." So she sails triumphantly into the verbal fray. A measure of Mrs. Peterkin's attitude toward the social worker is that Doll, an unsympathetic character, seems to be impressed by the white woman; and, as Mary's chief antagonist, she reveals both her bad manners and her obsequiousness when she says to the others, "If Si May-e had a walked in dis church befo dat fine lady from up-north, a-lookin like e looks I would a been so shame I couldn' a held up my head to hear what e was a-sayin'." Because of such abuse, Maum Hannah begins to weep; but Mary politely ignores these and succeeding remarks—for a while. After Doll taunts her about July, she loses her temper and draws a stern rebuke from Maum Hannah. But she is finally triumphant over the entire assembly when she looks her enemies in the eyes and says:

> "I know yunnuh talks about me behind my back, but I don' mind. Talk all you want to. I ain' no member o de church. I been baptized an' I been a member four different times in my life. A member, de same as you. When I git old an' tired seein pleasure, I'm gwine to seek and pray an' be a member again."
> She looked around and smiled.
> "If I was fat or either old, I might would settle down, but, tank Gawd, I qin' neither one. Not yet."[10]

At the beginning of the next scene, Big Boy, Andrew's son, comes to remind Mary of the motion picture of hell which is to be shown at the church that evening. Andrew, it seems, has relented in his persecution of both Mary and Budda Ben; and, when the two sinners enter the church that evening, Andrew greets them with a smile and invites them to sit near the front in the section usually reserved for the most devout. Then, while thunder and lightning fill the sky outside, the preacher begins to describe hell in traditional terms of fire, and the film begins. The crude portrayal of a Satan with horns, of tiny devils with pitchforks, and of souls that look like hop-toads is essentially humorous; but Mary is thoroughly frightened by the spectacle, as are other members of the congregation. All the women begin to scream, and curiously Doll is the most hysterical of all. Then, just when it seems likely that the church will be transformed into a charnel house littered with the bodies of the frightened-to-death faithful, the scene changes; Jesus appears on the screen: "a kind-looking white gentleman with a beard and long hair like a lady, all dressed in a long baptizing robe, [who] looked so harmless that everybody felt better at once."

The juxtaposition of these two filmed scenes is illustrative of the power which primitive religion holds for the plantation people— including such "realists" as Mary. Their fear of physical punishment is coupled with the promise of gentle mercy. The characterization of Christ is as ironic a portrait as Mrs. Peterkin permits herself—the effeminate white Jesus who is nothing more than "harmless." The promise of redemption to the congregation of Heaven's Gate Church, then, is primarily a promise to withhold punishment; and hell rather than heaven brings the blacks to the mourner's bench.

The rush forward after the film ends is frantic and swift—not only women and children, who are the most likely victims of fear, but big, broad shouldered sinners as well. As they pray, thunder shakes the sky; and, as Budda Ben worries about whether or not lightning will strike the church, Mary feels her first pangs of labor. In the comedy of misunderstanding that follows, Budda Ben thinks she is trying to get to the mourner's bench; and, when Mary shouts aloud for help, Andrew also thinks she is having a religious experience. Finally, Andrew—returning Mary's kindness twofold—realizes her predicament and drives her home in the raging storm.

The next scene continues in the humorous vein, but Mary's comeuppance is close at hand. After delivering twins, she is happy but tired and slips into a deep sleep. Later, she awakens to hear a baby's cry; and, after Maum Hannah determines that the crier is not one of Mary's infants, they discover yet a third baby hidden behind the organ. Maum Hannah, bewildered, asks Mary, "You reckon you could-a had dis chile and didn't know?" Mary denies the charge: "I know c ulti' me. No, Jedus. When I birth chillen, I know it." Then suspicion turns to the children, particularly to Seraphine, who has just returned unexpectedly from a long stay in the city. When Mary summons them all into the room—some little more than toddlers—and demands that one of them confess, they all stringently deny responsibility. Mary finally decides that she will just keep the third infant anyway since "Gal-chillen ain' de trouble boy-chillen is, nohow." When Doll comes to inquire about Mary the next day, Maum Hannah tells her that Mary has delivered triplets.

In the next chapter, however, Mary becomes suspicious of Seraphine, who will not eat and who mopes around the house all day, so she takes the girl into the woods and, after a long talk, learns the true state of things. Seraphine, like Mary, has been betrayed by her lover. Thus one of Maum Hannah's warnings has borne fruit, for, she has told Mary earlier, "If you keep on a-setting such a bad pattern to live by, befo you know it, one o you gals will walk straight in you tracks." Mary's spirit is not broken; in fact, she is not so much hurt by her daughter's misconduct as disappointed in her inability to rebound from the affair. No daughter of hers, she says, should be so discomfited by a mere man.

After administering a verbal chastisement, Mary threatens to tell everybody about the affair unless Seraphine pulls herself together. Then her voice softens and she gives her daughter some advice about the treatment of treacherous men: "Walk off proudful. Strut. Dat is de way to treat big-doins town men." She reminisces for awhile about July and her own first heartbreak, and then she tells Seraphine that she should look for new conquests. Mary has weathered the first blow with the same spirit that has carried her through the years of alienation from the church community: she is not as yet ready to submit to the yoke of conventionality. Her sins may be catching up with her, but she has enough love in her heart to embrace them and live with them in joy. The girl, who is finally ready to smile, throws her arms around her mother and says, "Si May-e, you's de best ting ever was, yes, you is. I love you too good, Si May-e."

The advice Mary has given Seraphine is put to the test in the next chapter when July, after twenty years of roaming, knocks unexpectedly at Mary's front door. She has been thinking about him only that morning (Mrs. Peterkin's somewhat crude preparation for his re-entry into the narrative); and, when she finally realizes who he is, all of her old love and bitterness rush back into her heart. Not only does he still have his good looks and his charm, but he also brings gifts and a wallet stuffed full of money which, he says, is all for her—except for ten dollars which he will give to Unex. Mary realizes that with her love charm—which she never was able to use on him—she could keep him for the rest of her life; and, for a moment, her head swims and her heart pounds. But she is no longer dominated by love or even the desire for comfort. The years have changed her from a fifteen-year-old romantic to the self-sufficient scarlet sinner; and, though there is still love in her heart for July, her pride is much stronger: "Take who back? You. July Pinesett? Befo I'd let you come inside my door, I'd see you rotted in Hell."

In language significant in its reference to damnation, she rebukes him and drives him from her door; but there are tears in her eyes and a lump in her throat for days afterwards. Maum Hannah comes to her and tries to persuade her to forgive the man, but Mary is adamant. The old woman points out that Mary has done little to deserve a perfect man, and this fact the younger woman is willing to admit; but she will not waver. Budda Ben comes to tell her about July's return; and, when he hears that Mary has turned the wanderer away, he too is unhappy with her: "I know, gal. I know how proudful you ever was. Too proudful." Once again, Mary rejects the advice that she herself has given earlier—in this case, to Budda Ben. Thus her independence has turned to willful pride which seems to invite punishment.

This chapter functions as a transitional one—a modulation in tone from the humorous to the pathetic. Mary's depression, while justified in terms of the reawakened memories she must live with, really serves as a preparation for the deep sorrow she is to experience in the next episode—the one in which her "proudful" spirit is finally chastened. Once again the scene is set up crudely. It is a stormy night and outside the animals are strangely unsettled. As Mary sits smoking her pipe before going to sleep, her eye falls upon Unex's picture; and she begins to speculate on his whereabouts and his fate. Suddenly there is a noise on the front steps, a loud knock at the door, and who should be there but Unex. He is soaking wet from the storm and has with him yet another grandchild for Mary to raise—a baby girl named Emma.

Mary agrees to take on the new responsibility as readily as she agreed to accept the burden of Seraphine's illegitimate child. In one sense this acceptance might be regarded as atonement for her own sins which have been visited upon her children. But, as Mrs. Peterkin points out in *Roll, Jordan, Roll,* children are considered lucky in a household, whether the mother is married or not. Not only do children prove to be a source of love and joy; but, more practically, they are also extra hands in the field and "old age insurance." On Blue Brook, the old agrarian pieties are still present in a way that they are not in the urban communities beyond the distant hills; and—in lieu of Medicare, social security, and other government-sponsored benefits—the young consider it a filial duty to take care of their parents and elderly relatives when they are too old to support themselves—even if doing so means receiving them into an already crowded one room shack. So the advent of one more illegitimate child into Mary's household is not something that she regards as either punitive or calamitous.

Unex, however, is grateful since the mother of Emma is dead and since he is unable to care for the child alone. In discussing this death, the conversation turns to the subject of burial expenses; and Seraphine explains the new "Bury League" on the plantation which includes the price paid out for each type of death: a child over twelve—$15; a baby under twelve—$12; a wife—$25; a lawful husband—$60. Seraphine adds that a common-law husband is not covered by the policy, and Unex expresses his dissatisfaction at such an unfair discrimination. Mary interrupts to say that she will not join the Bury League until she starts feeling ill; for, until that day comes, she will save her money for more immediate necessities and for pleasures.

This discussion serves at least one significant function in preparing the reader for what is coming since it shows Mary's utter confidence in her own vitality and in that of her children—a confidence that is soon to be destroyed. Just as she has talked about returning to the church at the last minute, so she talks about a last minute membership in the Bury League—just in the nick of time to avoid financial disaster. Her pride and self-sufficiency are for the moment set against nature itself, or perhaps God, rather than against the community of Heaven's Gate Church; and possibly for this reason she incurs a terrible punishment and returns to the church long before her interest in men and in pleasure has withered with old age.

The next morning Unex is ill with a strange malady—some sort of fever; and, as his condition worsens, Mary begins to fear for his life. Yet she still does not lose confidence in her own self-sufficiency; and, though Unex refuses food, she herself eats in order to pull him through with her own strength of body and character: "She would nurse Unex back to wellness, back to life. Death should not have him." But, when the night comes, even Mary's optimism gives way to resignation. Unex wakes with a shudder and tells her that he has the death rattle in his throat and that the final coldness is creeping up his legs. She asks him if he wants the church people to come and sing hymns, but he says he wants only her. She lies down beside him, puts her arms around his gaunt frame, and waits for the end: " 'Now, now,' she whispered in his ear, 'Si May-e is got you right in e arms. Don' be f'aid, honey.—Death ain' gwine to suffer you— no—all de worst is done over—shut you eyes, sonny, an' go sleep —' "[11]

There is no hint of religious piety in these words, no warning to repent or to pray for mercy; she is simply the Earth-Mother embracing her child and lulling him to the sleep of death with gentle words. She does not tell him that he will not die, only that the worst of his suffering is over; but, in his last moments, she tries by embracing him to use the warmth of her body and her love to stave off the chill of death. She herself then tries to pray; but to no avail, possibly because she has fallen out of the habit and possibly because the "natural self" within her dominates the religious one at such a time. She does not lose control; for, in the final moments of her son's life, she holds back the tears lest he hear them and be alarmed. Then he dies.

The experience overwhelms her; and she begins to moan softly, "not bawling, not beating her head against the wall as women do when they lose out in a fight with death. Sorrow had her dumb." For the first time, then, she has no retort, no defiant challenge, to hurl against the forces that pursue her. For something else is at work in her, something that is not in the same category as the moral strictures of the church community or as the pietistic gibes of old fools like Doll. Like April, Mary has come up against the ultimate powers; and, like April, she bows her head before them. Suddenly the old dichotomy of body and soul takes on renewed meaning for her. She has spent her years in a frantic preoccupation with things earthly; and now she must again consider the world of the spirit to which "her joy-child, her first-born, her jewel, July's son," has gone.

Only a few days earlier, Mary had dismissed the thought of death from her mind and the minds of her children; now she must face the reality of the grave. Although she had told both Maum Hannah and Doll that she would think about things spiritual sometime in the future when she had enjoyed herself to the fullest, she suddenly has to confront the problem as something immediate and demanding.

The contrast between the two worlds—the one she has too long forgotten and the one at whose shrine she has worshipped—now becomes all too apparent:

> She looked up at the sky where her precious child's soul was wandering about seeking its way to Heaven and God. The battered horn of an old red moon hung low above the dawn. The stars were pale and dim, poor lamps to light a lonely soul climbing that steep road trying to find its long way home.
>
> The earth lay still and black. The high sky might have the dead boy's clean soul, but the greedy old ground would get his body, his poor, thin, fever-wasted body, and turn it back into dust.[12]

Then the elaborate ritual of death begins which, along with the marriage or fertility ritual, is one of the chief ceremonies of every culture, primitive or sophisticated. The moan is the first outward and visible sign of grief, and Maum Hannah's cry, which is broadcast to the community at large, is as formalized and conventional as a cantor's or a muezzin's.

Oo——Oo——Ooo——Ee——Ee–Eee!
Oo——Oo——Ooo——Ee——Ee–Eee!

During the ritual, Mary is torn by guilt as well as by grief since she is certain she is the victim of divine retribution. But even in this condition, haunted by self-recriminations, she will not submit to the community at large. She has been brought low by it, and she will not give it the satisfaction of watching her collapse beneath the weight of her burden; so, as the ritual continues with the washing and shrouding of the body, she holds firm. But, when Andrew, whose kindness is a significant comfort to her, is about to board up the casket for the last time, she cries out her sorrow and acknowledges her Conqueror: "Oh, Gawd, why couldn' you le' me keep my child a lil bit longer?" Then she pulls herself together and moves to the church where the community has gathered for the services. There Doll's grief becomes so intense that she loses control; and, for a moment, the two enemies—the mother and the aunt of Unex—share a common sorrow. When the body is committed to earth, it is too late for the setting sun to insure a peaceful rest.[13]

Mary too can find no peace, alienated as she is from God's love. She finally considers the series of misfortunes that have befallen her children to be a judgment against her. The conclusion is a logical one which has been suggested earlier by Maum Hannah; since her sin has been scarlet and since the children were the fruit of that sin (including Unex, who was conceived out of wedlock), it follows that punishment for the sin be visited upon the children—that the fruit be blighted. Consequently, Mary concludes that "God had plagued her enough. She would pray until she found peace."

Thus, in her middle years, she must return once again to the role of the novitiate—the twelve-year-old who goes out alone, as does Missie in *Green Thursday,* and who seeks through prayer and renunciation a sign of salvation. Mary, however, has no easy time of it; for she has been too long the self-sufficient pagan. Once in the secrecy of the tall pines, she finds that the proper words and thoughts will not come to her. Like Faustus, she is too alienated from God to pray; and she is so close to despair—the unpardonable sin—that she bursts into tears and shouts aloud to "Jedus" for aid. Then, in the dawn of the day, her voice suddenly begins to speak the proper words; and the force of prayer is loosed within her. But this experience is not enough—not yet. "Seeking" is not an easy road—particularly for the hardened sinner; and she spends all day waiting for the sign which will signify God's forgiveness. She finally falls asleep toward evening, and the dream of salvation comes to her—and a dream that is almost medieval in its concept and allegorical in its significance. She sees Unex step out of an opened grave; he is weeping, and he points to a piece of white cloth on the ground upon which are ten red stripes, and he says "Dem scarlet stripes is Jedus' blood. Every sin you had laid a open cut on Jedus' back." When Mary looks questioningly, he speaks to her:

"You had nine chillen, enty, Si May-e?"
She had.
"All was born in sin, enty?"
She bowed her head low. But she had only nine children. Why were there ten stripes?
"Seraphine had a sin child, Si May-e."
She had.
"Gawd holds you responsible for Seraphine's sin. You set a pattern and Seraphine followed em. You is to blame."[14]

Before the grave melts and Unex vanishes, leaving only the bloody cloth, Mary learns from her son that she must pray until each of the stripes has turned to white. Mary begins to pray in her dreams—earnestly, one sin at a time; and one by one the stripes disappear. When she awakens, it is morning again; and Andrew is kneeling beside her, his face worn with worry and grief. Mary, however, is jubilant; and she tells Andrew that her soul is now clean: "E's whiter'n snow. Yes, Lawd, whiter'n snow." Andrew, in a significant gesture, leads her back to the Quarters (the community); and, in the final scene, he is instrumental in leading her back into the fold of the church.

Mary's reconciliation with God is, of course, the resolution of the main conflict of the novel—the conflict within Mary between her natural desires and her essentially spiritual nature. And it is significant that this resolution takes place in the woods, far from the company or help of others. Salvation, after all, is finally a matter of the state of Mary's inner soul—a matter to be settled between her and God. However, the final chapter closes with another kind of reconciliation—one which is less serious and perhaps more tenuous. Mary is invited to appear before the deacons—as is the custom in the black Baptist Church—in order to describe her vision and to argue its authenticity. Her final reinstatement into the church, however, is a matter for the deacons themselves to decide. As she prepares for this ordeal, she does so with something less than the humility of a thoroughly chastened supplicant. She may have been broken and humble before the wrath of God, but she knows the frailty of the earthly church too well to subjugate completely her pride or her sexuality. Thus she puts on her earrings and her love charm—those old symbols of the fleshly life she is promising to renounce. The deacons, she reasons, are after all no more than men.

In the congregation, Doll is watching both Mary and Andrew with sharp, worried eyes; and the two are to fight their final battle in this scene. When Mary tells her story with inspired passion, she directs most of her words to Andrew who is entranced by the spell of her eyes. And Doll is unsure whether charm or religious rapture causes Andrew's entrancement. But the other members of the congregation, like Andrew, are impressed by the sincerity of Mary's narrative. When she finishes, however, she finds that reintegration into the church community still has its obstacles; for Brer Dee, the head deacon, announces that she must be rebaptized! The theological absurdity of this decision is enough to alter the tone of the narrative from serious to humorous, and what follows is once again in the comic vein. Andrew stands and says that he has never heard of anyone being baptized more than once—that one time was certainly sufficient. Brer Dee says that the reason Andrew has never heard of the practice is because there has never been such a sinner as Mary. At that moment, Doll leaps to her feet to add that "[a]nother baptizing would do well if it rid Mary of all the sin she had."

For a moment, Mary burns with anger and hatred. Then, in a perfect example of Christian charity, she looks at Andrew's suffering eyes; thinks of "poor short-necked, short-waisted, short-winded Doll"; and begins to feel a surge of pity. The spirit of forgiveness that she has counseled Andrew to adopt is also working within her, perhaps as a manifestation of her revitalized Christian spirit, though it has been a part of her nature throughout the narrative. When the deacons rule that she must indeed go through a second baptizing, she meekly submits to the decision; but her earrings are still "gay and bold and shining." At the end of the meeting, everyone rushes to welcome her back into the fold; and the "reintegration" is complete—yet somehow on Mary's own terms.

The last person to congratulate her is old Daddy Cudjoe, who, many years ago, has given her the conjure rag that has held her in such good stead; and he makes a request:

"If you gwine to quit wid mens, now, Si May-e, do gi me you conjure rag. E's de best charm I ever made."

Mary looked straight into his eyes and smiled as she shook her head.

"I'll lend em to you when you need em, Daddy, but I couldn' gi way my love-charm. E's all I got now to keep me young."[15]

What does this statement mean? Has she really repented? Does she simply mean that she still wishes the admiration of the men in the community, or does it mean that she will take up her old ways when a good opportunity presents himself? Was the glint in Andrew's eyes something more than Christian charity? Does she still think that he needs a little straying from the straight and narrow path to make him a whole man again? All of these questions arise; but none is answered. Mary exists as an enigma—"saved" again, but whether or not "reformed" is anybody's guess.

III *In Summary*

Scarlet Sister Mary is Mrs. Peterkin's most successful novel, artistically as well as financially. Though April may be a more engaging figure in his pride and consequent downfall, Mary provides the reader with an exemplum that is finally subtler and more complex. For one thing, the conflict between pagan superstition and the Christian church is refined in this narrative in a way that places the novel within the context of the Western literary tradition without sacrificing any of the particularities of Gullah plantation life which are among the most striking fictional virtues of both *Green Thursday* and *Black April.* Mary's character is the epitome of the conflicting forces that operate within her community, and indeed the more sophisticated community at large. She is the superstitious pagan, the evangelical Christian, and the hedonistic individualist all at one and the same time; but her virtue, which is Christlike, derives from a loving heart rather than from superstition, dogma, or self-assertiveness. She is therefore, despite the occasional indulgence of her passion or her pride, a heroine in the fullest sense of the word.

The novel itself is more tightly structured than the works which precede it. Each scene has a definite function in the total movement of the narrative, and at no point does Mrs. Peterkin stop the action in order to catalogue or to lecture. Indeed, as suggested above, the comic action is classical in its complication, peripety, and resolution; and it is difficult not to believe that in the creation of this one work Mrs. Peterkin was the consummate artist, self-consciously controlling and ordering the inventions of the imagination. Even the diction and the syntax suggest the more complex and sophisticated vision of her subject matter that Mrs. Peterkin held before her as she wrote. *Scarlet Sister Mary* is a far cry from those first "crude" sketches that appeared in *The Reviewer,* but it retains all of the stark realism and primitive power that made those initial works so promising.

CHAPTER 5

The Vision Blurs

I *The Search for a Subject*

AFTER Mrs. Peterkin's surprising success with *Scarlet Sister Mary*, she remained virtually silent for four years since only a few stories appeared in magazines such as the *Saturday Evening Post* and the *Ladies' Home Journal.* Like many novelists who win the Pulitzer Prize, she suddenly found publication doors opening that previously had been shut; and she was able to sell her wares on the highest literary markets of the day. This new source of income might well provide a partial explanation for the lack of a full-blown novel to follow immediately the success of *Scarlet Sister Mary.* She was too busy making money.

In 1932, she published *Bright Skin*, the story of Cricket, a mulatto girl whose "mixed blood" causes her such hardship in the black plantation community that she finally renounces the world of her childhood and flees to New York; where she becomes part of segregated Harlem and the protégée of her grandfather, a black separatist. The poignancy of her troubled youth is complemented by the story of Blue, her "racially pure" cousin, who grows up to love his world; to marry Cricket; and later, after she has rejected him, to find comfort in another woman and in the fact that he is to be the foreman of the plantation.

When *Bright Skin* appeared, her publishers suggested that Mrs. Peterkin had deliberately taken such a long time completing the work in order to create a true masterpiece, a book surpassing all her previous triumphs. This statement seems to have implied that Mrs. Peterkin had become a self-conscious artist in the best sense of that phrase, that she was in some way now aware of a deeper obligation to her art then she had recognized in earlier and more productive years. It is possible that her success had affected her to the extent that she no longer regarded her fiction as composed for an audience limited to a locale or even to a generation and that she felt obligated to polish and refine her writing as she had never done before.

But the evidence of the book itself suggests another explanation for the long lapse between novels: Mrs. Peterkin had at last used up the literary resources at her disposal. She had written *Green Thursday*, a collection of linking short stories with definite overtones of tragedy; she had followed this initial effort with a powerful if imperfect tragic novel, *Black April*; and then she had crowned her development with a novel of rare comic vision, *Scarlet Sister Mary*; but the setting, most of the characters, even the scenes had been the same from book to book. All three books, however different the shape of the action or its essential meaning, were concerned with plantation blacks engaged in the archetypal experiences of birth, love, marriage, and death.

Such subject matter is of sufficient import to furnish a writer with fuel for his life's work—provided he is able to bring a fresh vision and an expanding consciousness to each new revelation of his world. Faulkner is the obvious example, and one could imagine him writing about Yoknapatawpha County into perpetuity without committing the sin of redundancy. Mrs. Peterkin, however, was not a William Faulkner; and her understanding of her subject matter seems to have been severely limited. Since she must have been aware of these limitations, her delay in bringing out a new novel may well have resulted from her desperate desire to break with the pattern she had established in her first three books.

It is also likely that the problem of the mulatto intrigued her and that she wished to record her view of the social enigma presented by his presence in a segregated society. She was not the first, of course, to exploit such a character in fiction. Mark Twain, William Dean Howells, and George Washington Cable were among the very few nineteenth century writers to broach this subject; several novelists had broken the ice for her in the 1920's; but even in the 1930's miscegenation was to many Americans, Northern as well as Southern, an extremely delicate matter.

II *Problems of Tact*

Though Mrs. Peterkin was one of the first to venture into such troubled waters, she did so with extreme caution. For one thing, the love affair which produces Cricket, the "bright skin" of the title, is spoken of only vaguely. The white man involved is left unidentified, but the author hints that he is a man of wealth and has a good name. The black woman who gives birth to the illegitimate half white daughter is described by her own kinsmen as rebellious and as given to wicked ways. Moreover, the wench is dead, a victim of her own folly long before the narrative opens. The sharp point of the theme in *Bright Skin* is also blunted by the fact that Cricket, the mulatto, is never depicted except as a denizen of the black community. She is not, for example, trying to "pass"—to live as a white in a white world. Nor is she shown as a latter-day Pamela in the ruthless employ of white men who continually launch assaults against her virtue.

Instead of the white community's providing the obstacles to her happiness, it is the black community that disapproves of Cricket's "tainted blood" and condemns her for the sin of her conception. Even at the end of the novel, when she finally escapes from the essentially conservative world of Blue Brook Plantation, she does not flee to a white society. She goes instead to Harlem in the company of a "black nationalist," there to fulfill her destiny by becoming a stripper in a black cabaret.

Finally, even within the black plantation community Cricket is never the victim of a tacit conspiracy which closes all doors to her. She is, in fact, loved devotedly by several of her kinsmen and playmates; she is kindly accepted by a good many more; and she is scorned by only a few—most of them people whose opinions are of little importance to her anyway. In fact, by the time she approaches adulthood, her "racial" problems have all but receded into the background, and the question is no longer whether or not the community will accept her; it is whether she will accept or reject the life that the community has to offer her. For it is within her power to be the most important woman on the plantation after she marries Blue, the heir apparent to the position of foreman. Yet she chooses to give up this future, forsake her husband, and in effect throw away the prize after the victory is won.

Thus, though Mrs. Peterkin dares to enter the lion's cage, one can never feel that the beast is really there as a danger. Little is risked; and, therefore, little is won. The reader is exposed, at the beginning of the book, to some of the pressures under which the mulatto girl must live in a homogeneous black community; but these pressures

are relatively mild and short-lived compared to the agonies of mulat-
toes in other novels, such as, for example, those of Amantha Starr in
Band of Angels.

III *Structure and Texture*

If the novel is so superficially concerned with the plight of the
mulatto, what then is it about? A close examination of the plot shows
that, in spite of herself, Mrs. Peterkin resorts to many of her old
characters and scenes and that they are embarrassingly reminiscent
of the earlier works. The book begins, as does *Black April,* in a
remote settlement up-river; and the point of view is immediately
established as that of Blue, an innocent backwoods boy who, like
Breeze in the earlier narrative, is about to make his first trip to the
plantation and meet the foreman—this time his grandfather, Cun
Fred. Blue's father is taking the son away from his mother because
she has proven a faithless wife; and in the parting of the boy and his
mother is some of the same poignancy that Mrs. Peterkin captured
in the earlier scenes of *Black April,* though the second treatment
suffers by comparison with the first.

Blue's father deposits the boy with Cun Fred and Aunt Fan and
then departs to make a new life elsewhere. Blue remains behind to
learn the ways of the plantation just as Breeze learned them; and,
when he fails to do well in his "lessons," he is soundly thrashed by
Aunt Fan, who is as stern a disciplinarian as Big Sue. Almost as soon
as he arrives, Blue meets two children about his age who are to play
significant roles in his life and in the action of the novel. The first is
Cricket, who is Blue's first cousin, the daughter of his mother's
sister. As she is pictured in the opening chapters, she seems an
innocent child of nature, more delicate and picturesque than the
robust blacks who surround her. One is almost reminded of Miranda
when Cricket appears for the first time, picking violets by a stream,
her hair hanging in a black cloud clear to her shoulders. But there is
some ugly talk about her origins which Blue overhears, and in Chapter Three he sees her playing near a ferocious boar—she is already
courting danger.

The second child Blue meets is May Jay, the "woods colt" son of
Blue's Uncle Wes and therefore another first cousin. Man Jay,
though lanky and raw-boned, has all the poise and know-how that
Blue lacks. He can plow all day without tiring, he can play a mouth
organ, and he has an easy way with Cricket that the timid, halting

newcomer envies. The groundwork is laid for the triangle which is
to develop later, and Cricket's final choice is perhaps foreshadowed
when Cun Fred remarks one day that Blue will someday be foreman. Cricket, despite the impropriety of her words, blurts out a
prophecy that is also a wish, "Not if Man Jay lives."[1]

In these opening chapters, another seed is planted that is to bear
fruit in the later action. When the children's common grandfather,
who is also named Blue, returns to a nearby town, he is calling
himself Reverend Africa and is preaching a gospel of black suprem-
acy and damnation for the white man. Reverend Africa will not set
foot again on the plantation which is a symbol to him of old humiliation; but he sends money to his father, Big Pa, and to Cricket; and
he invites them to come live with him. They both refuse, preferring
to remain on Blue Brook; but, years later, Cricket accepts his invitation and leaves behind her forever not only Blue but the world he
represents.

As foils to the three children and their developing relationships
stand such characters as Cun Fred, Uncle Wes, Aunt Fan, Bina, and
the two playmates Cooch and Toosio. Cun Fred and Uncle Wes,
replicas of Killdee and April, are proud, "womanizing" black men
whose self-sufficiency raises them above the common herd. Big Pa,
like Daddy Cudjoe, is an ancient figure still steeped in the magic of
the continent from which he came. Aunt Fan and Bina are reprises
of Big Sue and Sister Mary, and Cooch is remarkably similar to
Cinder. Toosio is a fat, self-indulgent nonentity. And all are minor
characters who play limited roles in the action.

Thus *Bright Skin* is really the story of the three children—their
initial friendship based on ties of blood, the inevitable rivalry between Man Jay and Blue for the affections of Cricket, the brief
victory of Blue, and Man Jay's ultimate triumph. These situations
form the raw material of the plot, and the reader is led to believe
that the essential theme of the narrative is racial in its overtones.
For, from the beginning, the older, more traditionally minded
blacks are harping about Cricket's white blood and the virtues of
racial purity. Blue is told by his father, Jim, while still enroute to
Blue Brook, that "a bright skin is a bad thing, son. Your Mammy's
sister birthed one and died." When the boy meets his grandmother
after reaching the plantation, she immediately inquires about the
color of Jim's children; when told they are black, she says, "Thank
God, Jim, your wife stuck to her race. Dat's better'n her brazen

sister done." And later she tells Blue, "You ain' no bright skin, Blue.
Thank God, you is black as de back of de chimney."

Cricket, who is constantly exposed to derogation from children as
well as from adults, adopts a defensive stance by flaunting her white
blood. Upon discovering that the characters in the reading primer
are white, she claims that she too will have a baby like the one in the
book; and, when Blue points out the racial difference, her reply is
pointed, "I ain' black like you." Later she wants to have a free
birthday party like white people instead of charging the children for
refreshments, the custom on the plantation. And, when the children
taunt her at her own party, she fights back valiantly, frail though she
is.

It is a difficult battle, however, and there are moments when
Cricket's courage fails her. In Chapter Ten, for example, a callous
discussion of her origins by the women of the community—a discussion that takes place in Cricket's presence—proves to be more than
she can bear. The humiliation is most intense when Jule, the mother
of numerous illegitimate children herself, says, "A bright skin ain'
got no place in dis world. Black people don' want em an' white
people won' own em. Dey ain' nothin but no-nation bastards."
When Aunt Missie finally sends Blue and Cricket away, the shaken
girl replies to her companion's cheering words with an admission of
defeat, "You's be down-in-de-heart too if you was a bright skin."
Later she tells Uncle Wes, her surrogate father, that she does not
want to be a bright skin and asks him about her mother, who she
assumes is in hell. The persecution of the ingenuous Cricket (which,
to some extent, bears out Jule's hard words) leaves indelible scars
and paves the way for her departure from the plantation at a relatively tender age.

Two other early scenes give additional dimension to the racial
theme and suggest something of the black's relationship to white
people, but that relationship is never graphically portrayed by Mrs.
Peterkin in any of her books of fiction. The first of these scenes takes
place when Blue and Cricket are sent to Cun Hester for a magic
bean to charm away Blue's wart. As Cun Hester shows them
through the Big House (she is the cook), the old woman denounces
the vanities of the white world while the two children listen in
wonder. She says, "Books is contraptions of Satan, Cricket. You
better leave em alone." When Blue asks who shot all the deer whose
heads grace the walls, Cun Hester replies, "De white gentlemen,

Blue. Dey minds run on shootin an' killin. No wonder God cut em all down." Cricket is curious about the white people for obvious reasons. "De white ladies wasn' mean like de gentlemen," she asks. "No, Cricket," Cun Hester replies, "dey was as sweet as a rose. But dey is lyin yonder in de graveyard most of em wid babies in dey arms. . . . Birthin' killed some, trouble killed the rest."

Then, as the children watch, she says a prayer to the sun, a chant which is obviously African in origin; but she brings to it a Christian emphasis, a Biblical rhetoric, and a South Carolina setting: " 'Oh, Master Sun, you day's work is done,' she prayed solemnly. 'You plowed you shinin furrow cross de sky. Now you is gwine down to rest.' Her eyes pressed forward as her voice strengthened. 'If all I done to-day be pleasin in dy sight—if you got a good report of me to give to de Great I-Am, give me a sign!' "[2] She gets her sign: a flock of crows caw in the twilight, and a chirping bird flits by the window; she is answered in her prayer with a response from nature itself.

As she continues her chant, she begins a kind of ritual dance, and the elemental forces seem to come alive for her: the sun shouts, the breeze sings, a cackle comes from the graveyard and is attributed by Cun Hester to the ghosts of white women. When Cricket remarks that the spirits should stay in heaven, Cun Hester announces their doom like an Old Testament prophet:

"Dey ain' went to Heaven. Satan fooled em. Poor creeters. Dey used to own all dis land. A narrow grave is all dey got now, an' dey have to share dat wid tree roots. No wonder dey laughs at dey-self."
"Why didn' dey pray?"
"Dey was too rich. Dey thought fine damask curtains an' tester beds could hinder death from layin his hand on dey hearts. Lord, how dey hated to die. Fast as dey went, dey spirits came back to de Big House. Even de trees is haunted. When de wind comes in from de sea, dat old gray moss pure weeps, de tree limbs pure moan and groan."
"You ain' scared of em, Cun Hester?" Blue shivered.
"Not me, son. Jesus is my captain, de sun is my shield. I been through many deep waters, but I face spirits same like people."[3]

In addition to beauty and eloquence, these passages have implications that are important not only for an understanding of *Bright Skin* but also of Mrs. Peterkin's other works. For here, stated unequivocally, is the black view of the white community that has been hinted at or barely defined in the earlier novels. This view is very close to that of the medieval Christian Church which deplored love of this world and which emphasized the joys of the next. According to Cun Hester, then, the black is superior to the white man since the black has suffered life's hardships and deprivation and since the white has lived in luxury. The black is Lazarus; the white man, Dives.

The second scene which sheds light on the racial implications of the novel involves Big Pa, who, like Cun Hester, is an old and devout black whose cultural roots are both African and Christian. As Blue and Cricket sit by the fire one evening, he tells them about the history of the Gullahs, of their tribal origins in Africa, of their treacherous capture by the whites, of their life on the plantation, and of their hopes for redemption through the sacrifice of Christ. He also ends his discourse with a prayer to the sun. Then he breaks down and weeps for the way of life he has left behind in Africa and for his mother, whom he will never see again. As he sobs uncontrollably, from the meeting house come the strains of a Christian hymn promising reunion with the dead:

> "I had a lovin mother,
> E's gone to Heaven, I know.
> I promised I would meet em,
> When de saints go marchin home."[4]

Despite the pathos of the ending of this scene, it serves much the same function as the one involving Cun Hester. The old woman's conversation serves to explain theologically the blacks' lot, while Big Pa's tale explains it historically. But the meaning is clear once again: it is the white man who has come to no good end, as Big Pa explains:

Before the war, the white people were vast-rich. They hunted, raced horses, fought chickens and pleasured from Christmas to Christmas. When they rode out, gold on the carriage and harness blinded people's eyes like lightning. The horses had eyes like coals of fire. Races sixteen miles long did not fag them for their breath was pure hot steam. When they came in sight, everybody ran and hid, for they trampled people down in the road like leaves. Lord, those were fine days. But war killed the old master, snake holes and crawfish ruined the trunks in the rice-fields, slime and weeds fouled the ditches. Everything went to ruin.[5]

The white people, then, have their day; but the Gullah, whose origins are noble (Big Pa is the oldest son of a chieftain), have a day that begins and ends in glory—as the Church hymn promises. The final breakdown at the end suggests the blacks' sorrow in this world, a sorrow which Big Pa and Cun Hester both accept as essential conditions of salvation; and, like many of Faulkner's more admirable characters, both black and white, their primary object in life is to endure—to learn to live with the conditions that life imposes and to do so with honor and courage.

Thus, in these two scenes, which appear to be little more than digressions from the main plot, one finds the key to an interpretation for the significant action that follows. The path of faithful acceptance is the way and the truth for the black. Salvation lies in remaining on the plantation and in taking what joys and sorrows life has to offer. Damnation lies in seeking fulfillment in the pleasures of this world which are most easily found in the far-off cities of the North. The joys and sorrows of the good life are illustrated in the chapters that follow, and Mrs. Peterkin reverts in them to former patterns with the description of typical plantation experiences, including some that have been dealt with before. Unfortunately, these scenes are neither so vivid nor so thematically relevant as those in the earlier books; and, for the first time, she completely loses control of her fictional materials. The racial theme, which she promises to pursue diligently in the first chapters, is all but forgotten in the pages which follow.

First, there is a scene in which Cooch is nearly burned to death. She recovers, however; and Cricket, who has won a book in a recitation contest, presents the prize to her injured schoolmate, thus effecting a kind of reconciliation with a persistent tormenter. Next, the hogs contract cholera; but the blacks, who butcher and eat them anyway, turn tragedy into triumph. Happiness is short-lived, however, because Uncle Wes—stabbed with an ice pick, conjured by his wife, and treated with boiling tea—grows violently ill and dies. His death breaks the hearts of the three children, all of whom love him like a father.

A good deal of space is then devoted to the funeral preparations and burial rites, and most of this material can only be described as "local color." There is, however, a curious parable of Jesus that emphasizes once again the superiority of the Negro's faith. Spoken by Cun Hester, it tells of a black Christ who performs miracles for the Africans and who then goes to the land of the white man where he is summarily crucified. At the end of the story, Aunt Fan asks,

"You reckon any white people is in Heaven, Cun Hester?" "Mighty few, Fancy," the old woman replies. "White people traded dey souls for dat fire an' food. Dey fetched black people to dis country an' learnt em sinful ways. White people has much to account for." And at that Big Pa breaks down again and sobs, "I wish I was back home in Africa."

Mrs. Peterkin then returns to the cycle of joy and sorrow—which is, to some extent, tuned to the seasons in an agrarian society. She describes harvest time, the abundance of nature, and the joy of the plantation folk during their brief prosperity. Not only are the crops in, but there are mullet, flounder, and sea bass in the waters, as well as crabs, oysters, and clams along the shore. For a while, the pain of death is forgotten in hard work and then in carefree celebration.[6]

These scenes are followed by a section devoted to the communal religious experience and particularly to the ritual of "seeking" which plays such an important part in the lives of the young. Like Missie, Breeze, and Mary, Cricket goes through a period of prayer and renunciation; and it is followed by a dream, or vision, which is considered a sign of salvation. These incidents achieve some sort of thematic significance when the deacons argue before the entire congregation that Cricket has dreamed an improper dream because, in addition to secular "reel songs," it contains white people. "Jesus," they remind everyone, "was black. Solomon said plain, I am black but comely." As they debate the case, Cricket, who has entered into the rite of seeking earnestly, doing so with the confidence of the "saved," suddenly falters. She announces to the assembly that, instead of a Baptist, she will become a Methodist like her dead mother. Aunt Missie is horrified, not only because the scripture prescribes total immersion, but also because Cricket's mother was a sinner. The scene closes with the Lord's Supper and with the foot-washing ceremony; and Big Pa suffers a seizure and dies in the midst of these solemn rites.

Big Pa's death, though thematically of little significance, serves as a punctuation mark to end not only the scene and the chapter but also the first section of the book, a section devoted to the childhood of the main characters—Cricket, Blue, and Man Jay. The next chapter begins with a transitional passage that summarizes a period of five years, one during which important changes have taken place on the plantation. For one thing, the Reverend Cato Singleton, a widower and a professed preacher, has risen to prominence in the community by opening a cafe where drinking and dancing are not only permitted but encouraged as proper Christian preoccupations. The plantation has also acquired a full-time "moonshiner" in Old Man Kelly Wright; he runs his own still behind the cafe and supplies Reverend Cato's customers with "white lightning." Much of the succeeding action takes places in the cafe, and the "moonshiner" plays an important role in the plot when he kills Cricket's lover in order to eliminate business competition.

The most significant change as far as the narrative is concerned, however, is the coming to maturity of the young people and the difference this evolution makes in their relationship. Thus, after rambling for the middle one hundred pages of the book, Mrs. Peterkin at last returns to the central action to depict the growing rivalry between Man Jay and Blue for the love of Cricket, who is now sixteen and old enough to marry. The addition of sexuality to the character conflicts does not alter their essential nature but merely adds intensity.

Cricket, for example, is still dissatisfied with life on Blue Brook and still wishes to escape; but she now has additional reasons to leave (since plantation men like Blue do not appeal to her) and also additional means to effect her departure. For she has become a desirable woman who is sought after by outsiders as well as by local men. At first, she believes that the best way to reach the world beyond and to succeed there is to seek education. Therefore, with Cun Hester's help, she writes to her white father asking for financial assistance; but, predictably enough, there is no reply; and, rejected by the white world as well as by the black, she settles back to wait for a different kind of opportunity.

Man Jay is also restless, as in his childhood; and he talks of going to town, of getting a job, and then of sending for his mother and Cricket. He even includes Blue in his plan, but the more tradition-ally minded youngster will have none of it and proudly announces that he will someday be foreman of the plantation. "Home is good enough for me," Blue says; but Man Jay disagrees and leaves to seek his fortune after committing Cricket to Blue's care. Blue is happy enough to accept the charge and urges Cricket to marry him, but her restlessness will not be stilled. "It ain' nobody here I'd marry to," she tells him. "I want to see how a town looks, Blue." And, "If I stay on here, Blue, nothin ain' ahead for me but to dry up an' get sour like Aunt Missie. If I marry you, Aunt Fan would say you married beneath you. I'm a bright skin, Blue. People here holds it gainst me. Cooch says bright-skin people stands well in town."[7]

The racial conflict has now been intensified by the sexual element and by the town-country conflict. The question becomes one of marriage as well as one of social acceptance; and, though Cricket is not really in love with Blue, she realizes that, even if she were, there would be tremendous obstacles to a happy life together. Thus it is no surprise when she is attracted to a rich mulatto who comes from the city, who drives an expensive automobile, and who sets up a still to serve the Reverend Cato's customers. The newcomer, whose dress and manners are sleek and sophisticated by plantation standards, takes Cricket away from Blue on the dance floor before the country boy realizes the danger; and within minutes the two have disappeared into the night. In a short time, their engagement is announced and their wedding day set; and Blue, obviously out-classed, attempts to find solace with Cooch.

Then, in a sudden twist of the action, Blue finds himself married to Cricket and close to attaining everything he has ever dreamed of. For the mulatto lover, though he is wise in the ways of the city, does not realize the dangers of the backwoods community where Skelly Wright, whose monopoly has been threatened, exists as a formida-ble evil. On Cricket's wedding day, the groom's peerless automobile is found abandoned in a cornfield; and Cricket's lover is nowhere in sight. When Cun Fred and the men of the plantation immediately suspect that the worst has happened, they convey these suspicions to Aunt Missie, Blue, and Cricket. The prospective bride faints when she realizes that she has been left at the church door; and Blue, in a gesture which is part altruistic and part selfish, offers to marry Cricket himself in order to save her from humiliation. Cricket hesitates, then accepts the proposal; but, after the wedding is over, she makes it clear to Blue that he may not enjoy the customary marital prerogatives. Shortly thereafter the dogs unearth the body of Cricket's lover, and Blue learns from Cooch that Skelly Wright is the murderer.

Like Joy in *Black April*, Cricket has entered into wedlock harbor-ing a guilty secret. She is already carrying the child of her dead lover; and, when Blue discovers the truth, he is both angry and humiliated. Since he has never consummated the marriage, he can be certain that the child is not his own; and his first impulse is to expose Cricket. But his love for her and his essentially gentle nature soon conquer this initial wrath, and he keeps the secret to the very end—even when he could use it effectively to win Cricket back from Man Jay. However, Blue does begin to seek pleasure outside his home; and Cricket watches him do so with understanding and forebearance. Finally, after Cricket loses her child and almost dies, there is a reconciliation; and the two begin a true marital relationship which seems for a short time satisfying to both.

But deep inside Cricket has not changed. Whether because of her years of oppression or because of her white blood, she cannot finally accept the black, earthy plantation worker that Blue typifies. When he comes from the fields, covered with dirt and sweat, she shudders with disgust; when he suggests that she enjoy herself at the cafe, she replies that she finds no pleasure in dancing with "black smelly mens." Blue is bewildered, but he attributes her dissatisfaction to the death of her lover or to the loss of her child. And Blue, even when she receives several letters from Man Jay, does not suspect that he is about to lose her. When the gifts begin to arrive for Cricket and when he sees her joy in them, he becomes jealous and journeys to the city in order to buy her something finer than the trinkets Man Jay has sent from Harlem. But, since Blue is fresh from the country, he proves himself an easy mark for pickpockets who steal all his money except a few bits of change.

Blue's experience, juxtaposed with the death of Cricket's lover, is really a reworking of an old fable, "The Town Mouse and the Country Mouse." There are pleasures to be found both in the city and on the farm, but there are dangers as well; and it is a wise man who keeps to the world he knows. The mulatto moonshiner is the city slicker who comes to the country and meets disaster, and Blue is the country boy who is fleeced by slickers when he goes to town. Even Man Jay, Cricket, and the Reverend Africa seem to be primarily oriented toward the city because their lives on the plantation can in some way be called failures.

Having tried the ways of the outside world, Blue returns home to discover that Cricket has left. At first, it appears as if she has only gone on a brief excursion with Aunt Bina; but, after time has passed without her return, Blue eventually receives a letter from Harlem saying that Cricket is happy there and wishes him to join her. By that time, however, he has entered into a relationship with Cooch—who gives him a larger measure of warmth and passion than Cricket had provided, and who is also pregnant and fiercely jealous over Blue's love for the mulatto girl. When he asks her for help in answering Cricket's letters, she takes the opportunity to insure that the marriage is destroyed by writing a letter of rejection.

The poignancy in the final meeting of the former childhood friends is marred to some extent by the interjection of some low comedy which might have been borrowed from the minstrel shows that Mrs. Peterkin so vehemently deplored. When Man Jay writes Blue that Cricket must have a divorce, no one on the plantation understands the meaning of the word. Blue finally consults with Cun Andrew who looks into his Bible concordance and who concludes that the word must be "diverse." He also decides that, since it is applied in the Biblical text to golden wine vessels, Man Jay must want Cricket to drink out of a gold cup. After much too much of this frivolity, Cricket and Man Jay arrive with a New York lawyer and explain the meaning of the word.

The final scene, though not without its moments of pathos, is a poor conclusion to the novel. Blue, realizing that he is about to lose Cricket, gets into a fight with Man Jay and is almost killed — saved only by Cricket's intervention. Then there is some talk of the Reverend Africa's fine tabernacle and night club, where racial intermixing is a nightly occurrence. Finally the lawyer reveals that Cricket has become a striptease dancer, and naked photographs of her are produced for all to see. Aunt Missie, horrified at Cricket's disgraceful conduct, rushes from the house; and Blue, after a painful conversation with Cricket, bids her goodbye forever. On the way home he is told that Cooch has presented him with twins.

Thus the action ends in a dissolution of communal bonds not unlike that to be found in tragedy. The family is torn asunder; and at the end two factions, living apart, are totally irreconcilable. On the one hand, Blue, Aunt Missie, Cun Fred, and Aunt Fan remain true to the old way of life. And on the other hand, Cricket, Man Jay, Reverend Africa, and Aunt Bina forsake plantation life for the glitter of the cities and, by implication, the type of society created and cherished by the white man.

But no one is really unhappy, despite the fact that all hearts have been severely wrung. Blue, to be sure, still loves Cricket; but he has found in Cooch someone who will be faithful to him and make him happy. He also has two children to give him hope for the future, as well as the promise that he will someday be foreman. Cricket and Man Jay, whose youthful years were a time of anguish, have at last found a world which will accept them and provide the wealth and excitement they seek. Both are, of course, ultimately rejected by the plantation community; but, since they do not want to live there, no great harm is done. In the final analysis, then, each of the main characters achieves some sort of social integration, but each is also aware that he is to some extent isolated. On this uncertain note, Mrs. Peterkin ends her career as a writer of fiction, though she was to publish a final book of nonfiction.

IV *In Summary*

Bright Skin is definitely inferior to the three earlier works of fiction, though there are scenes (e.g., Big Pa's reminiscences about Africa) which are as well wrought and powerful as the best segments of *Scarlet Sister Mary* or *Black April*. Indeed it is disturbing to realize that the prose in *Bright Skin* is probably more gracefully lyrical than any Mrs. Peterkin ever wrote. Yet as she perfected the textural elements in her work, her sense of structure and her inventiveness seemed to fail her. Written at a time when a demand was building for the fiction of social protest, *Bright Skin* failed to feed the growing appetite for antiestablishment tracts while at the same time offering no new insights into the nature of Blue Brook Plantation. The result, then, is a novel that neither breaks new ground nor explores familiar territory with greater skill and sensibility. It was a disappointment to her admirers and paved the way for a revaluation of her earlier successes which continues to this day.

CHAPTER 6

The Owl of Minerva

I A Work of Nonfiction

IN *Roll, Jordan, Roll,* her last volume,[1] Mrs. Peterkin is no longer
the writer of fiction, but the social historian and critic who tries
to explain the black to a readership that knows him only through
stereotypes and current slogans. In order to accomplish this purpose, she uses a number of conventional forms of discourse—
analysis, argument, typical description, illustration, narrative— and
her style, tone, and texture are different from the techniques
utilized in the fictional works. Her short simple sentences have
been replaced, in many sketches, by a complex literate prose. The
no-nonsense attitude of the author is evident in the more polemical
pieces which have little of the sentimentality or zealous rage that are
found in most contemporary discussions of the race question. And
the richness of detail that was characteristic of her fictional works
has given way to a spare economy that is suited to the needs of
formal discourse.

Roll, Jordan, Roll is composed of twenty-one "sketches,"
"dialogues," and "essays" that depict past and present life on the
Lang Syne Plantation. The volume is illustrated with seventy full
page photographs by Doris Ullman which, though poorly repro-
duced, depict typical plantation characters and scenes. Much of the
material is unique, since it is derived from firsthand experience.
Some of it is relevant only to the Gullahs—to their peculiar customs,
superstitions, and folkways; but a good deal more can be predicated
of the Southern black in general since the plantation experience was
the common heritage of virtually all blacks. Among the important
questions which Mrs. Peterkin discusses are the origins and nature
of the plantation, relationships between the sexes, the church and
religion, beliefs and superstitions, family ties, burial customs, and
the perennial cycle of plantation life.

Valuable though the book may be as a primary source for scholars (of the black in general and of the Gullah in particular), it has been largely ignored by the academic community. Mason Crum, for example, in *Gullah*, a study published by the Duke University Press in 1940, barely mentions Mrs. Peterkin; and other scholars are equally negligent. For the student of Mrs. Peterkin's novels, of course, *Roll, Jordan, Roll* has additional value. Though published at the end of her literary career, it serves as prolegomena for a full understanding of the earlier fictional works. She relates with precise and orderly arrangement the most important customs, beliefs, and attitudes of the Gullah people; and she presents a history and an analysis of plantation life which help to clarify both the setting and the enveloping action of the novels. In short, by exploring all the facets of Lang Syne Plantation, Mrs. Peterkin also defines Blue Brook for her readers.

II *Origins and Nature of the Plantation Community*

The first section, an essay, is both historical and anthropological in its intent. In it, Mrs. Peterkin discusses the institution of slavery, its effect on blacks and whites, and the black society that has evolved from the institutions and practices of an earlier era. The tone of the piece is typical of the author's individualistic attitude toward her subject, and idols topple right and left as she states in the plainest possible language her own version of Southern social history. Indeed, she succeeds by the middle of the second page in alienating both the implacable Confederate Fire Eater and the doctrinaire Yankee Abolitionist.

However tenuous some of Mrs. Peterkin's conclusions may be, this opening chapter of *Roll, Jordan, Roll* is one of her important contributions to the sociology and anthropology of the black, as well as a subtle key to her own attitude toward the fictional world she created. As an introduction to the pieces that follow, it provides a historical and anthropological frame for many of the character sketches, dialogues, and analytical studies which compose the loosely structured book.

Having analyzed the historical evolution of plantation life and its present structure, Mrs. Peterkin, in Chapter II, narrows her focus to the most important single figure in this unique society—the foreman. The piece is both a typical description and a character sketch of a particular foreman—presumably of Duncan, who was the prototype for several of her most successful characters, among them Killdee, April, and Cun Fred. She begins by talking about the foreman as a type—"a foreman who seems to fulfill the old African idea of chief of the tribe, meets with the utmost respect and his word is accepted as law." Soon, however, she is talking about a particular foreman; and the remainder of the sketch is composed of a series of anecdotes, some which illustrate generalizations about the role of the typical foreman and others which do no more than commemorate an interesting or amusing occasion. Several vignettes of the second type describe incidents that Mrs. Peterkin used in her novels and short stories.

In examining the sources of Mrs. Peterkin's fiction, it is interesting to observe how seldom she altered fact for the sake of fiction. It was just as she told interviewers time and time again: "Everything I write is true. Everything happened as I wrote it." And it is also worth noting that fact seldom obscures truth in Mrs. Peterkin's works. Her narratives are sifted and refined so that the thematic significance that emerges is rendered fully by her factual materials—a quality rarely found in fiction, much less in nonfiction.

III   *The Relationship Between the Sexes*

Chapter III is a dramatized dialogue between the foreman and a friend that concerns the joys and sorrows derived from women— with an emphasis on the sorrows. The short piece describes a skirmish between Jake and his wife Hester—a couple embroiled in the ancient battle of the sexes. Jake has been too sociable with the neighbors, and Hester accuses him of infidelity. When he becomes angry and strikes her, she dumps out the week's rations, destroys the washpot, and removes herself to her sister's house—depriving him of everything that a man expects to receive from a woman. At first he is too angry to care, but the next morning he thinks better of the situation; and, with some rationalization to save face, he hitches up the mule and goes to fetch her home. This short piece serves as the basis for a scene in *Scarlet Sister Mary*—the long dialogue between Mary and Andrew in which they discuss the defection of Doll. But this characteristic is not the only thing familiar about the story. Any experienced reader, male or female, will conclude, after reading the sketch, that the journey Jake makes is an archetypal one.

Chapter IV is a generalization about the passionate nature of the Gullah female which is followed by a long anecdote that serves as an illustration. "The women are frank about falling in love," Mrs. Peterkin writes, "and do not hesitate to let the man on whom their love alights know it, or to fight other women who interfere with their winning him." Then she tells the story of Jinny, who slashes her lover with a carving knife and then stands trial for the near-fatal assault. The action, the germ of a short story, has its climax when, after denying under oath that she has committed the crime, she becomes so enraged with her lover's cowardice in failing to testify against her that she can no longer hold her tongue:

"So, you is coward-hearted man, is you? You is scared to tell on me, is you? Well, den I'll tell de judge on my own-self." She turned to the judge, and lifted her voice: "I cut dat low-lived scoundrel, Judge, an e knows good as me I cut em. E'o a snake in de grass. De truth ain in em. E ain fitten to 'sociate wid no decent lady. An what's more, if I ever catch em walkin out wid dat black, slew-foot hussy to church or anywheres else again, I'll sure cut his coward heart out of em. I was easy on em dis time, but e better not cause me to lay hands on em again."[2]

Chapter V is one of those narratives that either bewilders or enrages the more sophisticated urban reader who is unfamiliar with primitive "backwoods" mores. Underlying the anecdote is a view of justice and propriety that is utterly foreign to the value system of contemporary America, but it is a part of the recent history of virtually every region in the country and still prevails today in many areas.[3] The sketch begins with a description of the relationship between a young white bachelor and his black manservant, both of whom, in their respective social circles, are lovers of fine horses and fine women. The young white "Cap'n" enters a local tournament, a half serious, half comic reenactment of a knightly combat; and the black becomes as emotionally involved in the contest as his employer. Fortunately, Mrs. Peterkin does not attempt to suggest any more than a passing resemblance between post-bellum South Carolina and King Arthur's England; and she concentrates on the black's elation over "Cap'n's" victory and on the unhappy consequences of too much post-tournament celebration.

The black has, it seems, taken a bride during his carousing; and the girl, a complete stranger, soon proves herself to be an unworthy character. Her distraught husband, perhaps as the result of the heady idealism toward women exemplified by the knightly "Cap'n" (the relationship between the tournament and what follows is ill-

defined at best), shoots and kills a rival who claims to be the father of
the wife's newborn child. The resultant trial, which seems to satisfy
Mrs. Peterkin as well as all parties to the incident (with the notable
exception of the dead man), ends in a verdict of not guilty. The jury,
whose deliberation is superficial, is apparently influenced by the
so-called "unwritten law" and by the speech of the black who trusts
the "Cap'n's" and the white man's justice. He tells Judge and jury
that "Me and de Cap'n ever had ways alike, suh. De Cap'n would a
done same as I done." Then he adds, "I reckon you woulda, too,
Judge."

IV   The Black Church and the Role of Religion
in the Plantation Community

Chapter VI is one of the most important in the book; and, as an
explanatory piece for the body of Mrs. Peterkin's works, it is particularly valuable. In this fifteen page expository essay, she briefly
touches on the history of the black church from Emancipation to the
1940's and then describes its present structure, its rituals, its mores,
and its peculiarities. The piece is by necessity sketchy, and she
seldom attempts to probe beneath the surface of an idea or practice
for its deeper significance; but much of what she describes is not to
be found in the published histories of the Southern Baptist or
Southern Methodist churches. Such histories usually do not deal
with the black church as a separate organization and seldom mention black membership except in brief references, footnotes, and
statistical charts. Mrs. Peterkin's essay might be regarded as a typical description reinforced by illustrations. From the beginning, she
discusses a particular Negro community (Lang Syne), but her comments are clearly about the typical Southern black church, though
some of the anecdotes are of local import only.

The author, whose religious views are tempered by a scientific
skepticism, obviously regards the emotionalism and sensuality of
primitive worship with less than complete approval. She indicates
her attitude with an anecdote about the cook who wreaked havoc at
a revival by jabbing one of the sisters with a hatpin. Her conclusion
is stated in explicit terms: "[T]his incident goes to prove that while
there is often real and earnest concern over religion, hysterical
emotions that have little to do with salvation are sometimes displayed."

Mrs. Peterkin ends her essay with two character studies of church
women. The first woman, a "lady sexton" in the Methodist Church,

deplores the sinful younger generation, misquotes scripture, and trains the Methodist children "so that they will not grow up to be ignorant like Baptists." The other woman, a devout Baptist, is admired by the lady sexton for she exemplifies the same religious attitudes and perseverance characteristic of her friend. These illustrative sketches are rendered with great affection and tempered by gentle humor. Despite some of their less favorable aspects, Mrs. Peterkin seems to have chosen the women to represent the best virtues that emerge from the Christian congregation—a community with which the author has not always dealt kindly in her fiction.

Chapter VII, in which Mrs. Peterkin reworks a sketch first published in *The Reviewer*, involves the old Methodist sexton and her Baptist friend, who is a "man-hater." This work is more than likely the approximate reproduction of a conversation that Mrs. Peterkin overheard during *The Reviewer* years when she was still an apprentice to the craft of fiction. It is interesting to note that the version printed here, though it is altered to complement the chapter before it, still lacks the sharp focus of her better pieces. The sexton tells her Baptist friend about nursing a dying woman and her inability to collect the promised fee from the bereaved husband. The piece closes with a visit from the husband who fails to mention the payment he has promised; instead, he seeks a sympathetic ear for his grief-stricken lament. This chapter, which contains some excellent dialogue in the Gullah dialect, touches upon such issues as the inevitability of death in the midst of life and the difference between services that can be "hired" and those that can only be voluntarily rendered.

Chapter VIII, one of the most remarkable in the book, contains a story told with the matter-of-fact simplicity of a fairy tale; and it is a tribute to the humility and strength of the blacks' faith. Though the narrative involves the miraculous, there is none of the ambivalence or irony that marks Mrs. Peterkin's fictional treatments of such occurrences. An elderly black woman who embarks on a marvelous adventure as a result of orders spoken by the "voice of God" is known in the community as "the Dreamer"; and she, the widow of a Baptist preacher, has left the church because "a voice" has told her the congregation is worshipping a false God. The voice also commands her to become a vegetarian, to renounce the wearing of conventional clothes, and to dress in robes made from white sheets. She is obedient to the word of God, and endures the scorn of the community because of her curious ways. Then she receives a command that is to take her from the midst of her friends and return her in glory.

Because her deceased husband has talked of Roman Catholicism, she is curious about the Catholic faith and makes endless inquiries about the subject. One night the voice tells her to go to Rome to warn the Pope that he is about to die. Terrified, she prays for guidance (lest the voice be that of Satan); and she again hears the command, this time with the additional order that her neighbor accompany her. When the community hears of her resolve to obey the voice, it tries to dissuade her and the neighbor who is also convinced of the mission's validity. The two women, firm in their resolve, sell their houses, go to New York, and board a boat bound for Italy. When they arrive, they are befriended by a kindly priest who arranges for their journey to Rome. There, though they are unable to see the Holy Father, they deliver their message and receive a purse from the priest who talks with them. As they are enroute home on another ship, word comes that the Pope has indeed died.

When they finally reach the plantation again, they have more money than they had when they started out—the financial result of the charity of sympathetic people on both sides of the Atlantic. In addition, they are both celebrities in a community which has formerly scorned them. The Dreamer spends her last years waiting for the fiery chariot that the voice has told her to expect, and one morning she is found dead in her cabin. She has presumably burned to death because her flowing robe has been consumed by flames, which, Mrs. Peterkin concludes, "made the chariot which took her spirit to heaven."

The piece deserves to be preserved, both as a parable of Christian faith and as an interesting example of occult adventure. Presumably the details are true; but, even if they are only legend, the purity of the narrative and its kinship to fable make it a valuable contribution to black folklore and unique in Mrs. Peterkin's works.

Chapter IX is less important as a genuine piece of scholarship than as a revelation of Mrs. Peterkin's own attitudes and opinions about a highly controversial question—that of the spirituals. So much has been written on this subject by scholars who have devoted their lives to the study of folk music that Mrs. Peterkin's essay must be relegated to the category of amateur speculation because, though she probably didn't know it, Mrs. Peterkin was venturing into deep water in broaching this subject. For example, when she maintains that the blacks' musical picture of life as hard and trying is the result of his terrible bondage in slavery, she has the support of many critics and scholars. But, according to others, these elements are just as frequently found in the earlier white spirituals; and it is simply a question of which came first. Since the arguments between scholars often seem to be motivated by ideological concerns, one of Mrs. Peterkin's statements in this chapter may be a perfect summation of the irreconcilable conflict between the opposing factions in what is surely an unresolved controversy: "Men forever believe what they need to believe."

V *Education and Superstition*

Chapter X is a character study of an older member of the Lang Syne community—a person whom Mrs. Peterkin calls "Uncle." In part, it is a typical description of the old ex-slave who deplores the irreverence of the younger generation, disapproves of modern conveniences, denounces the contemporary church as ruled by Satan, and mourns the dissolution of the white aristocracy. That such types existed is beyond question, but Mrs. Peterkin's sketch would be little more than the reintroduction of a worn-out stereotype had she not included a number of anecdotes which define Uncle as an irrepressible individual whose qualities of mind and character are unique.

For one thing, he is more highly educated than most of the older blacks and has been able to read and write since boyhood when he went to school with the children of his master. Such a practice was generally outlawed by a regime which feared that education would breed rebellion; but Uncle serves as an example that such an opinion was not universally held by the Southern plantation owners. He can recite the multiplication tables from "twice one are two" up to "ninety-nine times ninety-nine," he can "recite all the old blue-back speller without halting," and he can name every president and vice-president from George Washington to Franklin Delano Roosevelt.

His knowledge of history includes the discovery of America by Columbus, the Revolutionary War, and the Abraham Lincoln administration, one which he deplores. Lincoln, he maintains, was a troublemaker, "a white trash boy" who was elected high sheriff in Tennessee and then "went all around making speeches about how

white trash people were as good as anybody." The Civil War resulted from the reluctance of the people in the South to be ruled by
such white trash; and, when the South lost the war, the "scalawags"
from the North ruled the land; moreover, they proclaimed that
slavery was a sin, but they themselves had started the institution.
The source of Uncle's "historical account" is clearly the white community, and at times his facts are inaccurate; but his command of
details is remarkable. He has, for example, information about the
capture of the Gullahs, who, he says, were not fooled by promises of
red cloth and glass beads but had to be forcibly subdued.

He regards President Roosevelt as the reincarnation of Christ
whom God has sent to save the country from the Republicans—a
band of scoundrels bent on destruction. He warns, however, that
Mr. Roosevelt (he calls him "Rosebell") had better spend much of
his time in prayer because Satan (whose long history he can also
recite) slips out of hell every time God's back is turned and works his
mischief on the world.

The portrait of Uncle would be useful to those who deplore the
black's "psychological enslavement" at the hands of the white man.
But there is also evidence here to support the contention that,
though the slave was often "brainwashed," he was not always kept in
ignorance. Mrs. Peterkin's purpose, however, does not seem to be
related to the controversy over the intellectual life of the slave; she
is simply concerned with the truthful depiction of plantation life as
she knows it in all its complexity; and her rendition of the old man is
undoubtedly both accurate and affectionate.

Chapter XI is concerned for the most part with superstitions,
some of which are catalogued in the earlier works and some of which
Mrs. Peterkin writes about for the first time. Some of the superstitions which she cites are borrowings from the white community;
others are obviously the products of African culture. But Mrs.
Peterkin does not attempt to delve into the question of origins,
which is properly the province of experienced scholars; she is
merely the recorder, a role which suits her admirably; and the piece
is largely composed of short paragraphs loosely strung together.
They include superstitions pertaining to charms, cures, natural
phenomena, articles of clothing, religion, crops, creatures of nature,
supernatural spirits, and inanimate objects—a small treasure of
black folklore for the casual reader as well as for the learned scholar.

Chapter XII is the reworking of a sketch first published in *The Reviewer* which later was incorporated into the continuing action of *Green Thursday*. Originally titled "Roots Work," it is the monologue of an old black woman who recalls how her husband left her to run away with an orphan girl whom the couple had befriended and taken into their home. The situation is almost identical with that in *Green Thursday*, and the ending foreshadowed in the story of Missie and Killdee is revealed in "Roots Work." The husband, after wrestling with his conscience, finally leaves his wife and "takes up with" the teenager; and she bears him eight children over the twenty-three years they live together. When he dies, still estranged from his wife, the old woman grieves as if they had never been apart.

Chapter XIII is a companion piece to Chapter XII, and in more ways than one. The former is the complaint of an old woman who has lost her husband, and the latter is the lament of an old man whose wife and most of his children have been taken from him. In addition, both pieces deal with the efficacy of spells and conjures. The tale of the old woman is essentially pathetic, of course, while that of the old man, despite its grim beginning, is ultimately humorous. But these differences in tone serve to point up their complementary nature.

The old man's tale is rendered in indirect summary rather than through monologue, but many crucial words and phrases are quoted directly in order to capture the flavor of his speech. The first paragraph reveals that he is unhappy about his present status; and, when asked how he feels, he always replies, "poorly, thank God," "like old people," or "betwixt the sap and the bark." The old days, it develops, were prosperous and happy. His wife was good to him, as were various other women with whom he kept company; there were enough children to help with the work; and the fields and creeks were generous in their yield to him. This state of bliss ended, however, at one time: his wife died; boll weevils got into the crops; a tidal wave destroyed his hogs and cattle; and it also killed most of his children.

His chief complaint, however, is his second wife, who captured him through the use of magic. From this admission a comic tale unfolds that involves a fatal error in judgment that precipitates his downfall. A conjure bag is left on his step; and, though he takes some precautions to nullify its efficacy, he is not displeased since he believes it has been left there by a young woman whose attentions please him. Determined to court her, he starts out one evening, only to be sidetracked at the house of her mother, who is dressed in her finest clothes and seems to know he is coming. Before he realizes it, he is proposing; and only after he has married the woman does he realize who it was who actually left the conjure bag. Then it is too late, and he finds himself mated with "one 'scold gully' woman too old and too fat to work."

VI *Family Life and Parental Responsibility*

Chapter XIV concerns children—their status in the black community, their upbringing, their introduction to religion and the lore of the culture, the treatment of their ailments, and other miscellaneous matters pertaining to young people. Here it is interesting to note the contrast between the plantation community and the urban ghettos of today. On Lang Syne Plantation, many of the factors which have produced urban chaos are present. There is poverty, deplorable housing, inadequate formal education, considerable illegitimacy, and a matriarchal society in which the woman has to bear the burden of a large family because of the absence of the father who either has refused to marry her or has left her to fend for herself and the children when he has taken up with another woman.

Yet Mrs. Peterkin begins her sketch with the observation that "children bring good luck to a house, and a childless woman is pitied whether she is married or single." At first, this statement seems strange because at that time no governmental aid supported such deprived families. The reason, of course, for the delight in children lies partly in the very differences that distinguish this rural community of the early 1930's from the urban ghettos of the 1970's. In contemporary Harlem, children are an economic burden for the husbandless mother since they are too young to seek employment and need constant supervision to keep them from the inevitable dangers of big city streets and alleys. On Lang Syne Plantation, such children were a great economic asset and assumed at an early age responsibilities important to the agrarian economy. Mrs. Peterkin describes children, little more than toddlers, who follow along in the furrows the father has just plowed and who drop seeds that the mother and older brothers and sisters cover with hoes. The ones too small for even this activity "mind crows," a chore that consists of patrolling the new-planted furrows and of beating on pans or other scraps of metal to scare off the birds who might plunder the grain. Older children, who in a later time and in another environment might be joining street gangs, spend the early part of long hot summers clearing weeds from the fields with a hoe.

Thus, in the black community of Mrs. Peterkin's time and place, there was no plethora of unadopted children swelling the orphanages. Like Big Sue, Rose, and Killdee, adults were happy to have them around not only because of the work they could perform but also because they provided a kind of social security—insurance against the time when sickness and old age would overtake the foster parent. Of course, as the author points out, there was a genuine love for children as well as an economic motive for desiring them; but, as was also the case in the white community, the large families of earlier agrarian times were self-supporting and probably even prospered in geometric proportion to their increasing numbers. Such a supposition, of course, presupposed a sufficiency of good land and good farming conditions.

Lest this agrarian community sound too idealized, Mrs. Peterkin constantly emphasizes the point that plantation life was hard, on the children as well as the adults. Indeed, part of a young Gullah's training was the constant admonition to expect little from life and to bear adversity with faith and resignation. Such admonitions were reinforced with hard, cruel object lessons; and Mrs. Peterkin tells, as in "Teaching Jim," about the fire which burns the hands of those who play before it. "Black children are more dependable and capable than white children," she writes, because "pain teaches a burned child not to dread fire but to rule it."

Discipline, then, is the key to the doctrine of acceptance. The parents on Lang Syne are kind, says the author; but they are also severe when any sign of rebelliousness appears, against either parent or the religious view of life: "Tongues that lie or use bad words are washed clean with strong lye soap; pods of red pepper must be chewed to burn out mouths that give back-talk to grown people; disobedience is a grave offense, and a child that persists in it needs to be put into a sack and hung to a rafter and thrashed until blood leaks out and drains off the meanness that causes it."[4]

Besides its concern with discipline and virtue, Chapter XIV is specifically valuable to students of Mrs. Peterkin's earlier works because of the insights it provides into such diverse things as the

naming of children and the nature of "reel songs." This passage tells
the reader something of Mrs. Peterkin's method in naming her own
characters—

Deathless things, the earth, months, days of the week, fine wines which
white people drink, even cities, make good-luck names for firstborn sons.
Earth, Champagne, Sherry, February, March, June, July, Friday, London,
Charleston, are among the names commonly given.
A mother who named her boy children carefully nevertheless lost every
one when they began to teethe. She was so discouraged that she got a
"cunjure woman" to select a name for the next one she bore. The woman
named him "Try em an' see," and the baby lived and throve, although the
long name soon became "Tram-see."[5]

But it also explains the sources for many of the names of the
characters in her novels: April, June, July, Sherry, Poughkeepsie,
even Tramsee.[6]
    As for the reel songs, one begins to understand more fully the
church's banning of them after Mrs. Peterkin's description, which
is, alas, without the support of specific examples:

The reel songs, as the secular songs are called, express pretty accurately
the negro indifference to the white man's code of morality, but they are
great favorites with the children. Many tuneful melodies have harmless,
amusing words that tell of good things to eat, "greasy greens," "a chunk o'
fat meat," "sweeten-bread heavy as a maul," "shortnin' bread," "victuals
strong an' stout." Others that are frankly vulgar and indecent are sung just
as often without any apparent realization of impropriety, for the children
hear them sung constantly by grown-up sinners. All reel songs are barred
by the church, and any child past twelve years old must give up singing
them or stand in danger of hell. Twelve is the age of responsibility, when
the recording angel in heaven writes a child's name in a book and marks
down every sin against it. All worldly songs must be discarded then, not
only the reel songs but the songs that go with games.[7]

Chapter XV, a two page sketch, is in part illustrative of the desire
to have large families, as defined in Chapter XIV; but another idea
intrudes by the second page that runs away with the scene. The
principal character is an old man who has lived long, sown his seed
widely and abundantly, and lives with a third wife—a widow who
has brought eleven of her own children to live under his less-than-
ample roof. Because of the number of hands to do the work, the

family prospers; and he decides to build on to the house in order to make it more comfortable for everyone. The wife, however, apparently stricken with the desire for luxury, demands that he buy an automobile. He does so; and, because of the size of the family, they have to set up a schedule that permits everyone to take his turn behind the wheel. One day this tenuous arrangement breaks down, and the two families line up against each other and have such a terrible fight that the deacons of the church have to intervene in order to prevent outright murder. The wife and her family slit the tires of the automobile with a razor and depart from the premises. The old man concludes that "God knows single women and mules are so tricky they cause men to have sin, but the sin a widow-woman and a car can make is surely a token."

Once again, however brief, the piece has many of the virtues of a fable. The automobile—which may stand for material comforts, for progress, for any number of things—is such a force for evil that it can destroy a family that had striven together against natural adversity and had prospered. However unconsciously, Mrs. Peterkin's little vignette is a parable of what has happened to society as a result of this invention to which many social critics attribute the disintegration of modern family life.

Chapter XVI, a sketch about plantation courtship, concerns a "grader" in the asparagus packing plant who has been "conjured" by a pregnant girl he has forsaken. The theme of the narrative, somewhat vague, may be concerned with the unpredictability of the Lang Syne Gullah where affairs of the heart are concerned. In any event, the girl, the daughter of a respected deacon, is regarded by most of the plantation people as "brazen" and unworthy of the boy; for she is more like her promiscuous mother than her upright father. No one seems to feel that the "grader" has any obligation to marry her since he is now keeping company with a "nice mannersable girl." The people are worried, however, that the spell she has cast on him will prove effective because she is a "blue-gummed" girl and therefore capable of much meanness.

And their fears prove to be justified: he soon becomes violently ill and appears to be at the point of death. The boy's mother goes to see the old deacon and begs him to intercede with his daughter. His reaction is that of the outraged father who blames the boy for his shameless conduct and who vows that his daughter will never marry such a scoundrel. He says that he will stand by his daughter and help her to raise the child. Then, like Killdee in *Green Thursday*, the deacon brings the whole problem into the open by addressing all the asparagus packers and by repeating his denunciation of the boy. In the meantime, the grader improves and returns to work the next day, crediting his recovery to magical charms his mother has obtained. Soon afterward the baby is born, only to die. The baby's grandfather is grieved to distraction, but the mother seems strangely unmoved by the loss. There is some hint that she may have had a hand in the infant's death, but Mrs. Peterkin offers no explanation, and merely allows some speculation by the community.

The sketch ends with the engagement of the boy and the deacon's daughter, which is as much a surprise to the plantation people as it is to the reader. Was he "conjured" as July was in *Scarlet Sister Mary*? Did he love the girl all along? What does the deacon think? The answers to these questions are not even hinted at, and the reader is left with a sense of frustration—perhaps the feeling Mrs. Peterkin meant to convey. Whatever her reasons for telling the story, it is finally an unsatisfactory performance which barely deserves a place in an anthology of her finer sketches.

VII   *Last Rites*

In Chapter XVII, Mrs. Peterkin explains the "Bury League," a subject of controversy among characters in the fictional works. The organizational pattern, as Mrs. Peterkin describes it, is interesting in its complex and hierarchical structure. Each neighborhood has a local chapter of the organization, and each chapter is headed by a "Noble Shepherd" who collects the weekly dues and passes them along to the "Leader of the Flock," usually the undertaker who provides hearse, caskets, and headstones when the time arrives. The weekly dues, then, are really burial "insurance"; but the function of the Bury League goes beyond what one would expect from a conventional insurance company. Members, for example, are required to attend all funerals unless there is sufficient cause to do otherwise; and they must come dressed in their finest array. Thus, the older, simpler funerals were replaced by ceremonious rituals attended by large crowds.

And it is not pride alone that motivates the Negroes to prefer this new mode of burial. Mrs. Peterkin points out that fear is also a factor, a fear that stems from the ancient superstition that a spirit laid away without proper ceremony may wander restlessly across the face of the earth. She suggests that this belief is African in origin; but, since it is also an idea found in early European culture, it is difficult to say from which source it came into the Gullah community.

The final paragraph of this section deserves quotation because it is exemplary of Mrs. Peterkin's prose at its finest. Here, unhampered by the restrictions of point of view, she is able to describe the old graveyard in language that is simple in diction, yet sophisticated in syntax and in its subtle poetic rhythms:

Spring shows early in the tender, misty green of willows that mark the river channel where strong roots clutch swamp mud and strive to hold the unruly stream to its rightful road. Maples flame scarlet, poplars make bright yellow splashes, wood ducks quack gaily, turkey hens call gobblers who deserted them and their children in the fall to gang together all winter like carefree bachelors. Then the old graves sunken with waiting so long for Gabriel to blow his trumpet and clothe old bones with living flesh are sprinkled with blue violets; tangles of yellow jessamine drop gold bells and crab apple thickets send down showers of fragrant pink petals to lie among carved wooden heads of wheat placed on some of the graves long ago. Nobody knows who carved them or why the wood lasts so long, but everybody knows they are symbols of eternal life carved by somebody who believed that some day "the trumpet shall sound and the dead shall be raised incorruptible . . . and this mortal must put on immortality."[8]

VIII *A Faulkner Analogue*

Chapter XVIII, another of the *Reviewer* pieces, is a short story that in several respects bears a striking resemblance to William Faulkner's *Light in August*, which was published in 1932, eight years after Mrs. Peterkin's "Over the River" made its first appearance. The Faulkner narrative concerns Lena Grove, a simple, trusting girl who has an affair with a man and becomes pregnant. Since her lover, a sawmill worker, has left her, she decides to follow him, and does so on foot in the hot summer sun. She finally finds him; but, instead of marrying her and providing a home for their child, he rejects her; and she has her child in the house of a stranger.

In these significant details the stories are identical, but here the similarity ceases. In Faulkner's novel, the child lives and its mother endures, despite hardships and rejections; and she is still doggedly seeking the good life with every possibility of finding it. Mrs. Peterkin's heroine, who is additionally handicapped by the fact that she is deaf, is defeated by the circumstances; and, after murdering her own child, she falls into a deep fever and dies. Faulkner's story, then, is comic; Mrs. Peterkin's, tragic.

In many ways this piece is Mrs. Peterkin's bleakest view of human life. Even in *Black April*, where the hero is eventually destroyed by the forces which run the universe, some hope is left in the person of Breeze, who, like Lena Grove and many of Faulkner's other characters, remains to face the future—if not optimistic, he is at least durable. In "Over the River," all hope for the future is destroyed when the mother smothers the child because she is afraid that the hatred in her heart would poison the breast milk were she to feed the infant and thus make its death even harder. Having destroyed the new life she has brought into this world because she does not want it nurtured in hatred, she drags herself out of bed, buries the small body, and staggers back to the cabin where she has taken refuge and where she dies of fever as the worms swarm over her feet.

The narrative is effective enough, and Mrs. Peterkin is able to display some virtuosity in her handling of the point of view—which is that of the deaf girl. Her walk across the railroad trestle—with her inability to hear trains coming from behind and with her heaviness, which makes her steps uneasy on the crossties high above the river—is well told; and it extracts a good deal of the natural suspense from the situation, though not all of it. Also, the use of natural detail—as in most of Mrs. Peterkin's prose—is vivid and precisely described. And the toughness in the fabric of the narrative makes the story finally fall into the category of pathos rather than bathos.

IX   *The Cyclical Seasons: Toil, Sorrow, and Celebration*

Chapter XIX is an expository essay that is concerned with the Negro calendar year. Mrs. Peterkin begins with a discussion of the holidays which she says are identical with those celebrated by whites, except for Green Thursday (Ascension Day) which, for the black, is an important occasion. This day, she explains, derives its name from the fact that it always occurs on Thursday forty days after Easter when the earth is green; and she tells of the taboo against plowing on that day. Those who violate the stricture against such work risk a scourging by God—of the sort suffered by Killdee in "Green Thursday." The rationale for this kind of punishment is the indignity that the earth would have to suffer if it were tilled on the day it mourned the departure of Christ to heaven. Had Killdee gone fishing instead of plowing his field, he not only would have escaped the cruel fate that befell him (so goes the legend) but would also have had very good luck since on this day the moon is always right for fish to bite.

It is interesting and perhaps significant that, according to Mrs. Peterkin, the Gullahs paid little attention to any national holidays except those that have religious significance—Christmas, Good Friday, Easter. Thanksgiving is simply the beginning of the hunting season, and the Fourth of July is coldly ignored. Mrs. Peterkin's explanation is that both the Negro and the white communities have felt very little patriotic sentiment since the Civil War; therefore, they no longer hold the great Independence Day celebrations that they had had in ante-bellum times.

As for the rest of the calendar year, it is largely organized around the seasons and around the work or leisure that each brings. The end of the Christmas season, for instance, is the saddest day of the year because festive leisure is over, the year's work begins, and the labor ends only when crops are "laid by." Spring brings back a rise in spirits, not only because of the rebirth of nature's beauty but also because of the promise of money when the cotton comes in. Cotton-picking time is a period of prosperity when friends and relatives living in the city come home to enjoy the high wages and to have a reunion, albeit five days a week it must take place in the fields. As Mrs. Peterkin describes it, however, harvesting the cotton fields has its moments of satisfaction; the workers have a sense of pride that gives the work additional purpose. Thus, at the end of the day, the cheers are for those whose "sheets" are heavy with cotton, and jeers are for those who weigh in light.

As Mrs. Peterkin has mentioned earlier, cotton-picking time is also a period for revival meetings; for preachers come from everywhere to help save souls and to share in the bounty of the harvest. There is also much frivolous spending at the crossroad store since this is the only time of the year when the blacks have money for anything that might fall into the category of a luxury.

She concludes on a note of gaiety by describing the sinners of Saturday night and the sense of joie de vivre that seems to pervade the plantation despite the difficulty of the life there. There are those, of course, who might accuse her of glossing over the hard facts of the blacks' existence in her concluding paragraph when she maintains that plantation days "are never monotonous to these people who love life too well ever to find it dull." Yet in *Roll, Jordan, Roll* and in her other works she has not been one to minimize the struggle that the black must make in order to survive, nor has she suggested that the blacks' view of life does not have its melancholy side. She is simply saying in this essay, as she also did in *Scarlet Sister Mary,* that a certain spirit within the community makes these people a match for all the hardships they must undergo.

Chapter XX is a monologue in dialect which is spoken by a mother who tells someone—presumably the mistress of the plantation—that she has come to ask the carpenter to make a crutch for her little boy who has lost his leg in a cotton baling machine. A poignant vignette which emphasizes the mother's pity for her child and her pride in his perseverance, it was first published in *The Reviewer* and later appeared as a scene in *Scarlet Sister Mary*. In *Roll, Jordan, Roll*, it follows the sketch on cotton-picking time, possibly to indicate that after all there is another side to the picture that needs some attention—that, in the midst of flush times and celebration, there is also room for tragedy.

Chapter XXI, the final one in the book, is concerned with Christmas and with the unmitigated joy that fills the black community during this period. The holiday spirit lasts from Christmas Eve morning and through New Year's night, a period devoted to worship and jubilation. Mrs. Peterkin's description of the customs, delicacies, and religious rituals that comprise the holiday activities is, of course, in the long tradition of Christmas pieces that have been written by local colorists of all Christian nations. In fact, she is by no means the first to describe the black celebrations. Irwin Russell, whom Joel Chandler Harris called the first authentic portrayer of the black, wrote a long poem called "Christmas-Night in the Quarters" which touched on many of the same customs and attitudes that Mrs. Peterkin portrays.

Christmas for the blacks has its special charm, not only because of the religious significance of the holiday, but also because the crops have been gathered in. There is corn in the shuck, peas in the barrel, and meat in the smoke house, to say nothing of molasses in gallon jugs and hoards of black walnuts and hickory nuts. Christmas is a time of plenty, and there is leisure to enjoy the fruits of labor. In addition, everyone participates in the preparation for Christmas, and the community spirit that pervades all labor is one that has been all but lost in the white urbanized society of modern America. At the core of this spirit is the religious nature of the holiday and the unifying institution of the church that on Christmas Eve opens its doors and (to some extent) its heart to the brethren and the sinners alike.

As Mrs. Peterkin describes the worship services, they partake of two traditions—first, the larger tradition of the Western Christian Church with its Bible, its lore, and its rhetoric; and, second, the local plantation tradition, which involves the use of "old Mauma's" house as the "praise house," the seating arrangements of the faithful (up front) and the sinners (standing in the rear), the hiding of the sugar cane for the children's "chawing," the annual telling of the Nativity story, the midnight "shouting and singing" until dawn breaks on Christmas Day, and the last hymn of the service: "Jesus is born in Bethlehem! Peace on earth, good will toward men!"

The two traditions seem perfectly wedded on this occasion, and all the conflict that exists between the old tribal ways—including witch doctor, charms and curses—and the difficult theology of the Christian Church seems to dissolve in a burst of pure joy, which is primitive as well as holy. With this note of reconciliation, Mrs. Peterkin closes her commentary on black plantation life.

X *Conclusion*

In *Roll, Jordan, Roll*, Mrs. Peterkin has not averted her eyes from the hardships of the life these simple Gullahs live, but neither has she emphasized those hardships at the expense of the joys that are just as present at Lang Syne and just as real. To the end of her presentation she is honest in her vision; she is serving no social ideology and no political creed. There is not any hint of the reformer in her, nor is she attacking the idea of reform. As in her novels, she is as close to being the pure analyst as any modern commentator on black life has ever been; and she is more "objective" than any commentator is ever likely to be again. These sketches, essays, and vignettes are important social documents that embody essential lessons for a society embroiled in fierce racial conflicts that threaten to destroy its very fabric. If such works are not truth itself, they are the raw material of truth and as such demand to be studied.

CHAPTER 7

In Retrospect

I As a Literary Craftsman

DESPITE the neglect into which Mrs. Peterkin's work has fallen, she deserves consideration as a significant American writer. It would certainly be foolish to argue that she should be classified with great figures like Herman Melville, Hawthorne, Henry James, or Faulkner. Moreover, her fiction does not quite measure up to that of such modern Southern writers as Katherine Anne Porter, Eudora Welty, or Caroline Gordon. But Mrs. Peterkin has touched on subjects that no one else has treated: her Gullah plantation world, however restricted, is unique. And the technical skills she mastered were sufficient to give that world a proper and coherent form, one that seldom flaws the narrative for the discerning reader. This praise, perhaps, is small; but the statement is true of few American writers of fiction.

Despite the fact that Mrs. Peterkin was neither a Melville nor a Faulkner, her work, like that of such giants contains truths that belong to the ages. She was, to some degree, a writer for all time; and her fiction contains those archetypal experiences that are a part of human experience in any social or historical context: love, birth, death, the life-struggle, a vision of God and the moral order, the initiation, and man in conflict with society. These archetypes provide the thematic framework for the episodic plots she constructed.

To be sure, the weakest element in Mrs. Peterkin's fiction is the lack of sophisticated plot structures. While individual scenes in all the novels are beautifully shaped and are built to a climax with enviable skill, the overall action seldom exemplifies the same grasp of form. In one sense, *Green Thursday* is little more than a series of disconnected incidents—some of them redundant—which fail to coalesce into a meaningful whole. *Black April* is too loosely structured, and only near the end, when the story begins to focus on the tragedy of the giant foreman, does a pattern of order clearly emerge, an order which partially redeems the apparently careless choice of earlier scenes and incidents. Only in *Scarlet Sister Mary* is there a well-proportioned beginning, middle, and end—and the last is foreshadowed by the first; only in this one novel does the action seem to grow like a seed into full fruition. In *Bright Skin*, the looseness returns, and the focus of the novel is so imperfect that the reader cannot determine who is the main character, much less follow the strands of the several quasi-plots that are never quite woven into a satisfactory resolution.

However, in her depiction of vivid and credible characters she was probably at her best; and such portraits as those of Killdee, Breeze, April, Mary, Budda Ben, Cricket, and the magnificent Maum Hannah are testimony to her innate genius. But, despite these successful creations, she might have probed deeper. That she did not is probably attributable to the fact that she was unaware of the literary revolution that was taking place around her; for, during the 1920's and early 1930's, the American novel was in a period of transition. Such pioneers as Hemingway, Faulkner, John Dos Passos, and Fitzgerald were experimenting with techniques borrowed from European masters like James Joyce, or else they were creating their own innovations. Yet Mrs. Peterkin, though daring in her depiction of life's stark realities, was essentially conservative and conventional in the techniques of characterization.

While the stories of Gullah life that she was telling were acclaimed by eminent critics as "new," "different," "the first of their kind," her narrative methods were those used by writers in the late nineteenth century. Only her often childlike prose and the abundance of Gullah dialect, with its unique rhythms and exotic diction, give the texture of her prose a freshness that distinguishes it from that of a hundred lesser figures writing at the turn of the century whose style was more formal and "literary."

Her fragmentary sentences (some no more than a word) are perhaps an influence of Joseph Conrad, whom she admired above all other novelists; but a more probable explanation is that they are a conscious attempt to capture in essence the thought patterns of her characters and thereby to create a kind of subjective Realism.

Mrs. Peterkin is not so successful as her more famous contemporaries, however, because her central intelligence is seldom released from the bondage of the author and allowed to "go his own way." For example, the reader is vaguely aware that the sophisticated ordering mind of the author exists behind Blue or the sensual Sister Mary. Mrs. Peterkin never dips into "stream of consciousness"; neither does she ever absolutely commit herself to the limitations of her focal character's intelligence and sensibility. In this respect, she is closer to Thomas Wolfe's technique than to, say, Joyce's.

Still, one must admire her technical skill in at least one respect—her ability to make the Gullah dialect a viable vehicle for serious literature rather than to use it merely as a device to surprise or to entertain. Though she found the use of dialect distastefully tedious, she nonetheless felt it necessary to the verisimilitude of her characters. Consequently, she spiced much of her fiction with the peculiarly Gullah diction, grammar, and syntax. She did not, however, attempt to reproduce the dialect exactly as it occurred in the everyday talk of Lang Syne Negroes. Unlike many of her contemporaries who were also exploiting Gullah materials (Ambrose Gonzales and Samuel Gaillard Stoney, for example), she was not really concerned with linguistics per se. She seemed, instead, to be intent on capturing the flavor of the speech patterns in order to make her characters more credible rather than to leave behind an accurate transliteration of this unique American patois. Consequently, just as Killdee, April, and Mary speak a language of their own—one that lies somewhere between the true Gullah dialect and the more sophisticated speech of the Southern white community—Mrs. Peterkin creates the illusion of exact reproduction without the difficulty.

In the handling of dialect, then, Mrs. Peterkin resembles some of the finest writers in the modern literary tradition—Joyce, Frank O'Connor, Faulkner, to name a few; and she keeps company with these men for a very good reason. Like them, she is not so much concerned with capturing the quaint qualities of a regional culture as she is with treating human beings in universal conflicts—albeit human beings whose uniqueness derives in great measure from their local culture with its customs, attitudes, and language. Thus Mrs. Peterkin's modification of the Gullah speech gives an important clue to her true artistic motives; at the same-time, it suggests the nature of this strange dialect to readers who might never have heard its peculiar diction and lyrical cadences.

II *Portrayer of the Negro and His Culture*

In the late 1920's and early 1930's, at the height of her career, Mrs. Peterkin was regarded by many responsible critics as the finest contemporary portrayer of black life and culture. Indeed, among her most ardent admirers were such men as Walter White, Paul Robeson, and W.E.B. DuBois, all black activists, who praised her both in private correspondence and in public utterances for her fair and sympathetic depiction of the black community. She was also commended in most of the liberal journals by such ardent white champions of the black cause as H.L. Mencken, Carl Sandburg, and Joel Spingarn. Yet thirty years later she was being virtually ignored or else roundly condemned by the spokesmen for the intellectual left.

For example, in *Images of the Negro in American Literature,*[1] a book which surveys the scope of black fiction from ante-bellum days to the 1960's, one finds only a passing reference to the former Pulitzer Prize winner Mrs. Peterkin. And here Seymour Gross, the editor, is more interested in attacking the attitude of a critic who, according to Gross, finds in Mrs. Peterkin's work certain "racist assumptions" that link her with the very people whose influence she was attempting to counteract. Another recent critic, Willard Thorp, is more direct in his condemnation of Mrs. Peterkin; in contrasting her work with that of Dubose Heyward, he writes: "Heyward's pages are spotted with purple prose but Negro critics agree that his understanding of Negro life was remarkable. They are less enthusiastic about Julia Peterkin whose best-known work, *Scarlet Sister Mary* (1928), won a Pulitzer Prize. As the wife of a plantation manager, Mrs. Peterkin knew the Negroes of her region well, but in her later work she condescends to them and falls back on the legend of the happy, child-like Negro, content with a clean cabin and plenty of fat-back and pot liquor."[2]

Occasionally there is a brief and sympathetic reference to Mrs. Peterkin's fiction. For example, J. S. Ezell in *The South Since 1865,* after praising Paul Green, whose works were heavily laden with social criticism, says of Mrs. Peterkin: "She was probably a better interpreter of Negro life than Harris, although she did not create a

single outstanding character like Uncle Remus."[3] And historian
George Brown Tindall writes that her characters "were presented
with sympathy and respect but with an uninhibited candor. . . . "[4]
Perhaps the most revealing of these later evaluations, however, is
the one by John Bradbury in his exhaustive study of Southern fiction
published in 1963:

> Mrs. Peterkin's novels—all of them negro-bound—display an old Southern
> weakness, despite their basic intimate observation; her Negroes are rep-
> resented as curious phenomena with sensationally odd characters. The fun-
> damental traits she exploits are moral irresponsibility and savage supersti-
> tion. *Scarlet Sister Mary* gained wide reputation for its lurid mixture of
> sexual promiscuity, religion, and superstition, with authenticity guaranteed
> by its author's position as mistress of a large South Carolina plantation. But
> this novel in particular lacks conviction—*Black April* is perhaps her best. In
> none of her four books of fiction do basic economic and social problems
> figure, and white owners appear only as vague beneficent deities.[5]

Bradbury continues by suggesting that a later work by Nan Bagby
Stephen, *Glory* (1932), is in the same vein as Mrs. Peterkin's works;
and he describes *Glory* as "an exposé of Negro gullibility, flamboyance, and stupidity." Mr. Bradbury is also critical of Faulkner
for his racial attitudes, but he praises such writers as Paul Green and
T. S. Stribling, whose works are concerned with those economic and
social issues which Mrs. Peterkin ignores. This passage helps one
begin to understand the tremendous disparity between earlier
evaluations of Mrs. Peterkin and the more contemporary studies.
Current social postures provide the norm; and Mrs. Peterkin, pro-
gressive in her day, does not meet the standards set by more frankly
propagandistic writers. Her work does not picture the white man as
an exploiter; therefore, it is no longer a viable weapon in the struggle for black rights.

This view by Bradbury is open to several criticisms. In the first
place, Mr. Bradbury either has read Mrs. Peterkin carelessly or has
not read her at all. *Scarlet Sister Mary*, as indicated in Chapter
Four, is anything but morally irresponsible. The characters are
promiscuous, yes; but so are the saintly heroines of many modern
novels; and one suspects that, had Mary only been white, she would
have been recognized as that most popular and familiar of all contemporary fictional characters—the virtuous trollop. Then too, the
white plantation owners not only do not appear as "vague beneficent

deities"; they do not appear at all. They are totally absent from Mrs. Peterkin's four books of fiction. Occasionally the blacks may discuss the white people, as in one or two passages in *Black April* and in *Bright Skin*, but usually the remarks are gently disparaging: they are too puny to stand the climate; they will never get to heaven because they are overly self-indulgent. There are no white characters of consequence in any of Mrs. Peterkin's novels, and the ones who briefly "appear" are not owners—either of plantations or of Negroes.

Then, too, Mr. Bradbury fails to understand that in Mrs. Peterkin's works there are fictional values that have little to do with racial characterization. *Black April* is a tragedy; *Scarlet Sister Mary*, a comedy. The characters in these works are human beings caught up in archetypal experiences and conflicts that transcend racial strife, which is local and, one hopes, also temporary. Present-day critics of Mrs. Peterkin make the same mistake as her earlier champions when they regard her simply as a portrayer of racial stereotypes.

Finally, the critics Gross, Bradbury, Thorp, and others of like opinion apparently refuse to look at Mrs. Peterkin's works with any historical perspective. When Thorp says that Negroes are "less enthusiastic" about her, he must be talking only of more recent times; for no one was *more* enthusiastic than the Negroes of her own day. W. E. B. DuBois can hardly be called an "Uncle Tom," even by the standards of latter-day black militants; and he wrote one of the most complimentary of all the earlier reviews. Moreover, Mrs. Peterkin was subsequently invited to contribute to *Crisis*, the house organ of the National Association for the Advancement of Colored People.

The truth of the matter is that Mrs. Peterkin has fallen into disrepute for some of the same reasons that she enjoyed her earlier popularity. *Scarlet Sister Mary* was not widely received because of its "lurid mixture of sexual promiscuity, religion, and superstition"; but, when measured against the stereotypes found in the works of such people as Thomas Dixon, the black folk of Blue Brook seemed more sympathetically portrayed. These earlier writers were also interested in "economic and social problems," but Dixon was a blatant apologist for an economic and social system—that of the Old South; and his characters were devised to serve the abstract view of society that he held. Dixon was doing, in effect, what Mr. Bradbury and others believe the writer of black fiction should do. He fails in that he was not the right kind of economist or sociologist.

Mrs. Peterkin, on the other hand, fails, it seems, because she is not at all a sociologist or economist. Compared with the blacks of Shirley Ann Grau, T. S. Stribling, Paul Green, and others, her characters are less idealized than they ought to be; in their human weaknesses, they are made less noble and are treated with less obvious sympathy. A new stereotype has replaced the old, and by comparison Mrs. Peterkin is no longer in the forefront, but in the rear guard because in her works the stereotype is absent.

One of the most effective and relevant criticisms of this new approach to black fiction is that of Ralph Ellison, a talented and perceptive man of letters who is also black. Mr. Ellison maintains that the black experience in American fiction has been "distorted through the overemphasis of the sociological approach," and that those people who advocate or practice such a literature—i.e., one which attempts to view the black "predicament in exclusively sociological terms"—destroy the values in black culture "which are beyond any question of segregation, economics or previous condition of servitude."[6] James Baldwin makes much the same point when he writes: ". . . the failure of the protest novel lies in its rejection of life, the human being, the denial of his beauty, dread, power, in its insistence that it is his categorization alone which is real and which cannot be transcended."[7]

That Mrs. Peterkin would agree with Ellison and Baldwin in condemning the kind of fiction Mr. Bradbury seems to advocate is clear from her own critical statements on the subject. In an article for the *North American Review*—which was only incidentally a review of Lyle Saxon's *Children of Strangers*—she provided critics who care to know with a rare insight into her ideas about the black as a fictional character. While defending Saxon's sympathetic and realistic treatment of a quadroon, she launched an attack on other Southern writers, mostly from the previous generation, who were intellectually dishonest in their depiction of the black, the very people with whom she is now being equated. Her indictment— which could well be the preamble of a literary credo—is broad enough to cover all fictional use of ethnic stock characters, including Jew, Irishman, Scot, or Southerner. Predictably, she focuses on the popular black stereotypes prevalent in the short stories and novels of the late nineteenth and early twentieth centuries, and she classifies them into three main types:

The most popular one showed loyal, grateful slaves, or ex-slaves who were devoted to the families of their present owners and eager to sacrifice themselves for their white friends. Another prized portrayal presented the Negro characters as amiable, carefree comic figures, full of easy laughter and always ready with a gay song or amiable dance step. A third well-known presentation showed the Negro as a drinking, gambling, worthless creature who was such a menace to white civilization that he spent most of his days on the chain-gang until he was finally lynched by a mob of white citizens resolved to protect white society from injury at his hands.

These patterns of Negro conduct were emphasized in literary productions so persistently that they were accepted as authentic. And not until comparatively recent times have our dark-skinned neighbors been treated as individuals, as human beings whose position in the social scale is complicated by problems and difficulties not found in the lives of their white contemporaries.[8]

It was against such stylized and unimaginative portrayals of the Negro that Mrs. Peterkin was reacting when she began to write her own sketches in the early 1920's. To a great extent, her attempt to render the South Carolina Gullah in purely Realistic terms led to her fame as a novelist. Indeed, the stereotypes in Mrs. Peterkin's fiction are present only by implication; they hover on the brink of possibility like gray ghosts to provide a contrast with the colorful flesh-and-blood characters she creates. April, with all his arrogance and nobility, is set in bold relief by the shade of Thomas Nelson Page's obsequious servant; Budda Ben's bitterness is grimmer because of the frantic good humor of Mr. Bones; and Scarlet Sister Mary's virtue is at least partially defined by antithesis in the inflammatory rhetoric of the revived Ku Klux Klan. That Mr. Bradbury and others fail to recognize this truth seems a pity.

There are, of course, a few critics and scholars who have devoted some time to an examination of Mrs. Peterkin's works and therefore appreciate their intrinsic merit. But, alas, the best studies are unpublished; they rest on the bookshelves of graduate research libraries where they gather dust. There is, for example, an excellent master's thesis at the University of Georgia which contains a wealth of biographical material and some important critical insights. Another thesis at the University of South Carolina concentrates on Mrs. Peterkin's use of folklore. A third, at Stephen F. Austin College, though limited in value, treats the author's realistic depiction of the Gullah.

Perhaps the most definitive unpublished work is a doctoral dissertation written at Florida State University by Louis L. Henry. This study is particularly noteworthy because in his few critical comments, Mr. Henry is not reluctant to point out what he considers to be Mrs. Peterkin's weaknesses, despite his basically sympathetic point of view.

III   In Summary

At the moment Mrs. Peterkin is all but forgotten; and her fiction, when it is discussed at all, is usually dismissed as either malicious or trivial. The hue is definitely not the wear. Admittedly, at her best she was no more than a star of lesser magnitude in the South. But she was admired by millions when few others were shining; and time, her present enemy, may prove in the long run to be a faithful friend.

The earliest rebirth of interest in her work, however, may come in the fields of sociology, folklore, and history, where she has much to offer the serious scholar. Certainly her portrayal of plantation life has a ring of authenticity that is lacking in most modern fiction on the subject; and since she was often more reporter than literary artist, she is all the more valuable as a primary source for historical research.

Both *Black April* and *Roll, Jordan, Roll* are priceless collections of black folklore and contain much material that bears close examination. Once again her artistic failures become positive virtues to serious students in the field. The tedious initiation of Breeze into plantation life is, at the same time, a compendious catalogue of Gullah attitudes on a variety of subjects; and the loose structure of her last major work allows for a more overt examination of black folkways than would otherwise have been possible. To be sure, these books are not, in and of themselves, examples of good scholarship; but they are certainly the raw material for more thoughtful investigation.

And one can envision a day—far in the future, to be sure—when historians will be able to look at the South dispassionately enough to see its essential complexity. To such excellent sages, Mrs. Peterkin will surely be a more reliable authority than Thomas Nelson Page on the one hand, or Erskine Caldwell on the other; for she lived in the interregnum between the tyrannies of two mythologies; and for a moment in time, with the scales of opinion perfectly balanced, she wrote honestly and clearly of what she knew to be true.

Notes and References

Chapter One

1. Medora Field Perkerson, "Julia Peterkin—Author and Farmer," *The Atlanta Journal Sunday Magazine*, April 28, 1940, p. 1.
2. The Negroes who lived on Lang Syne plantation were known as "Gullahs," a term whose origins are at best obscure. One theory holds that the word is a corruption of "Angola." Another maintains that the name is derived from the "Golas," a group of tribes which inhabited the West African Coast from which most South Carolina and Georgia slaves were imported.

Their language, also known as "Gullah," has its own syntactical patterns, its own peculiarities of pronunciation, and a unique disregard for standard English inflections. In addition there is a vocabulary peculiar to the Gullah speech, though authorities are at odds over how much is African in origin and how much is merely a corruption of words essentially English in origin. Such scholars as John Bennett, George Phillip Krapp, Ambrose Gonzales, Reed Smith, Guy Johnson, Mason Crum, and Samuel Gaillard Stoney maintain that the vocabulary is almost wholly borrowed. Lorenzo Dow Turner, however, in his remarkable study, *Africanisms in the Gullah Dialect* (Chicago, 1949), lists literally hundreds of Gullah words which he traces back to native African languages. His evidence is impressive and, indeed, persuasive.

3. Louis L. Henry, "Julia Peterkin: A Biographical and Critical Study" (Doctoral dissertation, Department of English, Florida State University, 1965), p. 151.
4. Perkerson, p. 1.
5. *Ibid.*
6. Emily Clark, *Innocence Abroad* (New York, 1931), p. 213.
7. *Ibid.*, p. 218.
8. *Ibid.*, p. 221.
9. Marilyn Price Maddox, "The Life and Works of Julia Mood Peterkin" (Master's thesis, Department of English, University of Georgia, 1956), p. 10.
10. Clark, p. 223.

11. Letter from Mrs. Peterkin to Joel Spingarn, in Joel E. Spingarn collection, Manuscript Division, New York Public Library.

12. Julian R. Meade, "Julia Peterkin," New York *Herald Tribune*, January 17, 1932, p. 5.

13. *Ibid.*

14. Clark, p. 224.

15. Maddox, p. 8.

16. Clark, p. 224.

17. "Again a Serious Study of Negroes in Fiction," *The New York Times Book Review*, September 28, 1924, p. 8.

18. Maddox, p. 39.

19. W. E. B. DuBois, "The Browsing Reader," *Crisis* XXIX (December 1924), 81.

20. Clark, p. 226.

21. Undated letter from Mrs. Peterkin to Joel Spingarn, in Joel E. Spingarn collection.

22. Letter from Edward F. Krickel to the author, October 13, 1970.

23. Clark, p. 221.

24. Maddox, p. 41.

25. Grant M. Overton, *The Women Who Make Our Novels* (New York: Dodd, Mead and Co., 1928), p. 259.

26. Letter from Mrs. Peterkin to Anne Johnstone, March 1927, in Bobbs-Merrill correspondence file.

27. Letter from Mrs. Peterkin to D. L. Chambers, March 1927, in Bobbs-Merrill correspondence file.

28. John Crowe Ransom, *The Fugitive* I (April 1922), 1.

29. Donald Davidson, *The Spy Glass: Views and Reviews. 1924–1930*, (Nashville: Vanderbilt University Press, 1963), selected and edited by John Tyree Fain, p. 23.

30. Letter from Stark Young to Julia Peterkin, dated "Sunday," circa 1927, quoted in Maddox, p. 46.

31. Unsigned editorial, *The State*, July 3, 1927, p. 4.

32. Letter from Julia Peterkin to E. K. Chambers, May 1927, in Bobbs-Merrill correspondence file.

33. Charles M. Puckette, "On a South Carolina Plantation," *The Saturday Review of Literature* III (March 19, 1927), 660.

34. Robert Herrick, "A Study in Black," *The New Republic* LVII (December 26, 1928), 172.

35. John W. Crawford, "Hound-Dogs and Bible Shouting," *The New York Times Book Review*, March 6, 1927, p. 5.

36. Clark, p. 215.

37. Letter from Julia Peterkin to E. K. Chambers, August 23, 1927, in Bobbs-Merrill correspondence file.

38. Herschel Brickell, "A Pagan Heroine," *The Saturday Review of Literature* V (November 3, 1928), 318.

39. Herrick, p. 172.

40. Ben Wasson, review (untitled), *Outlook and Independent* CL (November 21, 1929), 1212.

41. Joseph Warren Beach, *The Twentieth Century Novel* (New York, 1932), p. 232.

42. Roark Bradford, quoted in a letter from Anne Johnstone to Mrs. Peterkin, November 8, 1928, in Bobbs-Merrill correspondence file.

43. Edgar Kemler, *The Irreverent Mr. Mencken* (Boston: Little, Brown and Co., 1950), p. 215.

44. Henry, p. 85.

45. Maddox, p. 66.

46. Henry, p. 89.

47. John Chamberlain, "Mrs. Peterkin's New Novel of Negro Life," *New York Times Book Review*, April 10, 1932, p. 7.

48. Archer Winston, review of *Bright Skin, The Bookman* LXXV (April 1932), 108.

49. John Chamberlain, New York *Times* (December 15, 1933).

50. Letter from Mrs. Peterkin to Mrs. B. A. Behrend, July 22, 1940, in the Behrend collection, Clemson University, Clemson, South Carolina.

51. Letter from Mrs. Peterkin to Mrs. Behrend, July 16, 1940, in the Behrend collection.

52. Letter from Mrs. Peterkin to Mrs. Behrend, January 29, 1942, in the Behrend collection.

53. Letter from Mrs. Peterkin to Mrs. Behrend, March 29, 1954, in the Behrend collection.

Chapter Two

1. Clark, p. 221.

2. As in Faulkner's *The Unvanquished*.

3. In a section which probably should have been printed as a prologue to the entire collection rather than as part of "Ashes."

4. Clark, p. 219.

5. Julia Peterkin, *Green Thursday* (New York, 1924), p. 11.

6. *Ibid.*, pp. 103–04.

7. *Ibid.*, pp. 111–12.

8. *Ibid.*, p. 132.

9. *Ibid.*, p. 137.

10. An inconsistency. Here Daddy Cudjoe is pictured as an outsider to the church community. Later in the book, he appears as one of the congregation.

11. *Green Thursday*, p. 164.

12. *Ibid.*, p. 188.

13. *Ibid.*

14. A. E. Housman, *Complete Poems* (New York, Henry Holt and Company, 1959), p. 89.

Chapter Three

1. Julia Peterkin, *Black April* (Indianapolis, 1927).
2. Northrup Frye, *Anatomy of Criticism: Four Essays* (Princeton: Princeton University Press, 1957), pp. 33–34.
3. *Ibid.*, p. 37.
4. One of the few white characters in Mrs. Peterkin's novels. He appears only briefly and is nameless.
5. *Black April*, p. 156.
6. *Ibid.*, pp. 214–15.
7. *Ibid.*, p. 267.
8. *Ibid.*, p. 278.
9. *Ibid.*, p. 279.
10. *Ibid.*, pp. 306–07.
11. *Ibid.*, p. 314.
12. *Ibid.*, p. 316.

Chapter Four

1. Frye, p. 43.
2. Not permanently, at any rate. Of course natural disaster often disrupted the community temporarily.
3. Julia Peterkin, *Scarlet Sister Mary* (Indianapolis, 1928), p. 19.
4. *Ibid.*, pp. 52–53.
5. *Ibid.*, pp. 54–55.
6. *Ibid.*, p. 82.
7. *Ibid.*, pp. 201–02.
8. *Ibid.*, p. 219.
9. *Ibid.*, pp. 240–41.
10. *Ibid.*, p. 325.
11. *Ibid.*, p. 326.
12. *Ibid.*, p. 326.
13. An African superstition which was prevalent among the older Negroes and rejected by the newer members of the Bury League, who preferred their funerals on Sunday afternoon.
14. *Scarlet Sister Mary*, pp. 335–36.
15. *Ibid.*, p. 345.

Chapter Five

1. Julia Peterkin, *Bright Skin* (Indianapolis, 1932), p. 54.
2. *Ibid.*, p. 117.
3. *Ibid.*, p. 119.
4. *Ibid.*, p. 139.
5. *Ibid.*, p. 136.

6. It is clear in *Bright Skin* as well as in *Black April* that Mrs. Peterkin is describing a coastal rice plantation rather than one located, like Lang Syne, farther inland.
7. *Ibid.*, p. 233.

Chapter Six

1. Except for a few articles and speeches. *A Plantation Christmas*, published as a clothbound booklet in 1934, first appeared in *Country Gentleman* many years earlier.
2. *Roll, Jordan, Roll* (New York, 1933), p. 54.
3. Particularly in the Southwest, as a careful reading of any Texas newspaper will reveal.
4. *Roll, Jordan, Roll*, p. 176.
5. *Ibid.*, p. 184.
6. Lorenzo Dow Turner argues in *Africanisms in the Gullah Dialect* (Chicago, 1949) that the Gullahs also have secret names which they never reveal to the white community.
7. *Roll, Jordan, Roll*, p. 179.
8. *Ibid.*, p. 219.

Chapter Seven

1. Seymour Gross, "Introduction," *Images of the Negro in American Literature* (Chicago: University of Chicago Press, 1966), p. 6.
2. Willard Thorp, *American Writing in the Twentieth Century* (Cambridge: Harvard University Press, 1960), p. 259.
3. John Samuel Ezell, *The South Since 1865* (New York: The Macmillan Company, 1960), p. 289.
4. George Brown Tindall, *A History of the South* (Baton Rouge: Louisiana State University Press, 1967), vol. X, p. 308.
5. John M. Bradbury, *Renaissance in the South: A Critical History of the Literature, 1920–1960* (Chapel Hill, 1963), p. 83.
6. Ralph Ellison, "That Same Pain, That Same Pleasure: An Interview," in *Shadow and Act* (New York: Random House, 1964), p. 23.
7. James Baldwin, "Everybody's Protest Novel," *Partisan Review* XVI (Spring 1949), 585.
8. Julia Peterkin, "One Southern View-point," *North American Review* CCXLIV (December 1937), 397–98.

Selected Bibliography

PRIMARY SOURCES

(Listed in the order of publication)

1. Books by Julia Peterkin
Green Thursday. New York: Alfred A. Knopf, 1924.
Black April. Indianapolis: Bobbs-Merrill, 1927.
Scarlet Sister Mary. Indianapolis: Bobbs-Merrill, 1928.
Bright Skin. Indianapolis: Bobbs-Merrill, 1932.
Roll, Jordan, Roll. New York: Robert O. Ballou, 1933.
A Plantation Christmas. Boston: Houghton Mifflin, 1934.
The Collected Short Stories of Julia Peterkin. Frank Durham, ed. Columbia:
      University of South Carolina Press, 1970.
2. Short Stories, Sketches, Poetry, Reviews, Speeches
"From Lang Syne Plantation." *The Reviewer* II (October 1921), 6–9.
"The Merry-Go-Round." *Smart Set* LXVI (December 1921), 69–72.
"Imports from Africa." *The Reviewer* II (January 1922), 197–200.
"Imports from Africa. II." *The Reviewer* II (February 1922), 253–59.
"Studies in Charcoal." *The Reviewer* II (March 1922), 319–27.
"The Right Thing." *The Reviewer* III (April 1922), 383–88.
"A Baby's Mouth." *The Reviewer* III (May 1922), 437–42.
"Silhouettes." *The Reviewer* III (June 1922), 500–03.
"Missy's Twins." *The Reviewer* III (October 1922), 668–73.
"From a Plantation." *The Reviewer* III (July 1923), 925–31.
"Venner's Sayings." *Poetry* XXIII (November 1923), 59–67.
"Over the River." *The Reviewer* IV (January 1924), 84–96.
"The Foreman." *The Reviewer* IV (July 1924), 286–94.
"Daddy Harry." *The Reviewer* IV (October 1924), 382–83.
"Maum Lou." *The Reviewer* V (January 1925), 17–32.
"Manners." *The Reviewer* V (July 1925), 71–80.
"Whose Children?" In *The Borzoi 1925*, pp. 155–64. New York: Alfred A.
      Knopf, 1925.
"The Sorcerer." *American Mercury* IV (April 1925), 441–47.
"Vinner's Sayings," *Poetry* XXV (February 1925), 240–43.

"Negro Blue and Gold." *Poetry* XXI (October 1927), 44–47.
"Seeing Things." *American Magazine* CV (January 1928), 26–27, 115–16.
"Proudful Fellow." *Century* CXVI (May 1928), 12–22.
"The Ideal Woman for a Man-Made World." *Book League Monthly* I (March 1929), 5–10.
"Heart Leaves." *Saturday Evening Post* CCII (October 5, 1929), 5, 153, 154, 156.
"Greasy Spoon." *Ladies' Home Journal* XLVI (October 1929), 5, 139, 141.
"A Plantation Christmas." *Country Gentleman* XCIV (December 1929), 24, 86, 87.
"Santy Claw." *Ladies' Home Journal* XLVI (December 1929), 20–21, 163, 165.
"The Diamond Ring." *Good Housekeeping* XC (June 1930), 28–31, 170, 173, 174, 176, 177, 180, 183.
"What I Believe." *Forum* LXXXIV (July 1930), 48–52.
"Ashes." *Golden Book* XIII (June 1931), 51–55.
"The Art of Living." *The State*, June 6, 1933, p. 2.
"A Plantation Christmas." *Scholastic* XXXVII (December 14, 1935), 4–6.
"One Southern View-point." *North American Review* CCXLIV (December 1937), 389–98.
"Ashes." *Ellery Queen's Mystery Magazine* XXIII (March 1954), 81–89.
"A Plantation Christmas." *Good Housekeeping* CLI (December 1960), 54–55.

SECONDARY SOURCES

BEACH, JOSEPH WARREN. *The Twentieth Century Novel.* New York: Appleton-Century-Crofts, 1932. One of the few serious commentaries about Mrs. Peterkin's fiction technique.
BRADBURY, JOHN M. *Renaissance in the South: A Critical History of the Literature, 1920–1960.* Chapel Hill: University of North Carolina Press, 1963. Excellent example of current attitudes toward Mrs. Peterkin's fiction. The critic fails to view the author's work with any historical perspective and discusses her as a portrayer of the black rather than as a novelist concerned with archetypal human experience.
CHENEY, BRAINARD. "Can Julia Peterkin's 'Genius' Be Revived for Today's Black Myth-Making?" *Sewanee Review* LXXX (Winter 1972), 173–79. A perceptive analysis of the present intellectual climate and its relationship to Mrs. Peterkin's literary reputation.
CLARK, EMILY. *Innocence Abroad.* New York: Alfred A. Knopf, 1931. The founding editor of *The Reviewer* devotes one chapter of her book to Mrs. Peterkin. She provides the reader with an intimate personal portrait of the authoress during her formative years and quotes from a number of revealing letters.

COKER, ELIZABETH B. "An Appreciation of Julia Peterkin and *The Collected Short Stories of Julia Peterkin.*" *South Carolina Review* III (June 1971), 3–7. An assessment of Mrs. Peterkin by a friend and fellow South Carolina novelist.

CRUM, MASON. *Gullah.* Durham: Duke University Press, 1940. Study of the history, culture, and peculiarities of the low-country black. Excellent prologomena to an understanding of setting and enveloping action in Mrs. Peterkin's fiction.

DUBOIS, W.E.B. "The Browsing Reader." *Crisis* XXIX (December 1924), 81. A review of *Green Thursday* by the militant black leader; attitude exemplifies the earlier enthusiasm of liberals for Mrs. Peterkin's sympathetic portrayal of the Gullah.

DURHAM, FRANK. "Introduction" to *The Collected Short Stories of Julia Peterkin.* Columbia: University of South Carolina Press, 1970. This collection is principally valuable because it includes most of Mrs. Peterkin's short stories and sketches. There is also a lengthy "appreciation" by Durham and some biographical information.

GUESS, WILLIAM FRANCIS. *South Carolina: Annals of Pride and Protest.* New York: Harper and Brothers, 1957. History of South Carolina with several pages devoted to Mrs. Peterkin's career. One of the few critical commentaries which strikes at the heart of Mrs. Peterkin's essential value as a writer of fiction.

HENRY, LOUIS L. "Julia Peterkin: A Biographical and Critical Study." Doctoral dissertation, Department of English, Florida State University, 1965. Most definitive work on Mrs. Peterkin. Emphasis is primarily biographical and historical, but there is some incisive criticism as well.

MADDOX, MARILYN PRICE. "The Life and Works of Julia Mood Peterkin." Master's thesis, Department of English, University of Georgia, 1956. Well-written, sympathetic study of Mrs. Peterkin's life and career. Because the authoress cooperated in the preparation of this study, there is a wealth of original material included. Invaluable source.

MORROW, LENNA VERA. "Folklore in the Writings of Julia Peterkin." Master's thesis, Department of English, University of South Carolina, 1963. A fine examination of this aspect of Mrs. Peterkin's work.

TURNER, LORENZO DOW. *Africanisms in the Gullah Dialect.* Chicago: University of Chicago Press, 1949. Brilliant study of Gullah speech that has implications far beyond the field of linguistics, since it reveals much about the survival of primitive culture in the black community.

Index